This was the way the sporty fifties driver outfitted an Austin-Healey 100M: a tasteful number of badges, and twin driving lights. The folded windshield was something Donald Healey insisted on.

Motorbooks International Illustrated Buyer's Guide Series

Illustrated
Austin-Healey
BUYER'S GUIDE™

Richard Newton

Motorbooks International
Publishers & Wholesalers ®

First published in 1984 by Motorbooks International Publishers &
Wholesalers Inc, PO Box 2, 729 Prospect Avenue, Osceola, WI 54020 USA

© Richard F. Newton, 1984

Motorbooks International is a certified trademark, registered with the
United States Patent Office

Printed and bound in the United States of America

The information in this book is true and complete to the best of our
knowledge. All recommendations are made without any guarantee on
the part of the author or publisher, who also disclaim any liability incurred
in connection with the use of this data or specific details

Library of Congress Cataloging in Publication Data
Newton, Richard F.
    Illustrated Austin-Healey buyer's guide.

    1. Austin-Healey automobile—Purchasing.   I. Title.
TL215.A92N48   1983   629.2'222   83-13250
    ISBN 0-87938-104-3 (pbk.)

Cover photograph: Austin-Healey 100-4, by Andrew Morland

Motorbooks International books are also available at discounts in bulk
quantity for industrial or sales-promotional use. For details write to
Special Sales Manager at the Publisher's address

ACKNOWLEDGMENTS

Over several years, and several books, I've had the opportunity to work with a lot of different marque clubs and the Austin-Healey groups have a lot more fun than most people. Not only do they love their cars, but they do most of the work on them themselves, and they never take themselves too seriously. Anyone who owns an Austin-Healey and doesn't belong to at least one of these clubs is missing something. This book surely couldn't have been done without them.

One of the realities of writing a book is that no one does it alone. It takes the help of a lot of people, and in the case of the *Illustrated Austin-Healey Buyer's Guide* it took the help of several Austin-Healey clubs.

When it came time to read through the chapters George Harrison; George Garbut; Thomas Kennedy; Rob Morrow; Paul Woglom; Pete Morrison; Joe Pepe; George Null; Ken Walsh; Norman Nock; Chuck Gowan; John Bertanzel; Lynn Cline; Charles Harper, Jr.; John McNees; Walt Manberger; Tom Blake; Gregory W. Hunter; Shelley Gelbaum; R. Wayne Reynolds; Dave and Priscilla Hooper; Peter Genovese and Roger Gimbernat were all a tremendous help.

These are people who know and love Austin-Healeys— people who are only too happy to help new owners. Then there was Mike Cook of Jaguar who allowed me to dig out the old Austin-Healey pictures from the files up in New Jersey. Also, my wife, Elizabeth, who read through several drafts of this book, should get a lot of credit for the fact the book is written in understandable English. Without all of these people, the book couldn't have been written.

TABLE OF CONTENTS

INTRODUCTION

An Austin-Healey was the car you bought when you had out-grown your MG. It was the car you bought when you couldn't afford a Jaguar. It was never the car of the white wine drinkers and the quiche eaters. It was always a little bit uncivilized and it always seemed to have a little too much power for the chassis sophistication it offered.

An interesting thing is that which Healey you prefer probably depends a lot on how old you are. People might not remember their first sighting of other cars, but they almost always remember the first time they saw and, more importantly, drove an Austin-Healey. For a lot of people this was the six-cylinder version. But if you're a little older, or a collector, then it's the four-cylinder car you want.

Still another group of people are fondest of the Sprites, the affordable sports car of the sixties. No matter what year Austin-Healey you want in your driveway, it's the reminder of an earlier time that you want most.

Austin-Healeys are linked to an era that Donald Healey understood as well as any man. Healey always had a flair for taking a rather mundane set of car parts and assembling them in a new way, a way that gave them flair and totally transfigured their humble beginnings. The way he usually did this was to take someone else's transmission and engine and a lot of suspension

This was the first Healey sports car. This two-seater was called the Healey Silverstone. It used the standard Warwick Healey chassis and suspension, which was the basic chassis that was used in a number of Healey cars after the war. Healey used 2443 cc engines, and gearboxes from Riley in these cars. Jaguar Cars, Inc., photo.

parts, and place them on a chassis of his own design. The final step was to cover the mechanicals with a flowing body. Healey's first production car was produced in 1946 and labeled simply the Healey.

By one of those freak accidents of fate, Donald Healey (bound for America to explore export markets) found himself on the same ship with the head of Nash-Kelvinator, Mr. George Mason. By the time the ship landed in New York their discussions had gone beyond a mutual interest in photography to the idea that Nash might very well be interested in adding a two-seater to its model line. The result was a proposal to use the Healey Silverstone chassis with Nash running gear and call the car the Nash-Healey. It brought Nash engines, transmissions and rear axles together under a Healey body. In April 1950, the prototype rolled out of the shop. These first cars were all bodied in England by a firm called Panelcraft. After 1952 they were built by Pininfarina, of Italy, before being shipped to North America. The Nash-Healey was short lived and perhaps one of the ugliest of the postwar period.

By 1951 Donald Healey had decided the real market was in developing a cheaper car that would still be fast. The same idea was also making the rounds in the Triumph offices. It was no mere coincidence that both the TR2 and the Austin-Healey were designed for the American market. They were really American cars—manufactured in England, but built for Americans.

A 1954 Nash-Healey coupe; a roadster body style was also available. Built from 1951 through '54, the Nash-Healey was powered by a 235 ci ohv straight-six. American Motors Corporation photo.

The Austin-Healey was an American car in the sense that Donald Healey tailored it to what he believed Americans would buy. An Austin-Healey is much rarer in England than it is in the United States. Almost eighty-nine percent of all the big Healeys built were exported to the United States; under six percent of them were sold in England.

Thus, you'll find that it is generally easier to find parts in the U.S. than from English suppliers. It also means that your chances of finding a good Austin-Healey are far better in the United States than anyplace else on the face of this earth. When the major Healey clubs in the colonies hold a meet, they actually have more cars present than exist in all the garages of England.

When it comes to the appreciation of the cars' values, the story gets even more interesting. The big-buck cars are the 100S and the 100M, with the 100S leading by quite a margin. Prices seem to be increasing on a regular basis, although so few of them change hands in any given year, no one really knows for sure.

The 3000's went up in price right after the last ones rolled out of the Abingdon factory. Their prices then stabilized for a few years and now seem to be going up once again, although not at such a steep rate. These are the cars for the mature Healey fans; they have elegance, carry people in comfort and are great fun to drive.

Austin-Healeys are one of the best buys on the postwar collector market. When the whole range of Healeys is considered, just about any type of car you might want is in the lineup. You can have a two-passenger, open car with a huge, torquey engine, all sitting on four delicate wire wheels. You can have a touring car with a fine walnut dash and elegant center console—just the thing for a quick run into the city from your country estate. When you feel whimsical, the Bugeye Sprite is just the thing to make you laugh as you drive down the road.

The best part of all is that the cars are really affordable. There is no such thing as an Austin-Healey priced out of sight. People didn't buy Austin-Healeys for speculation, they bought them to drive. This means that average people can still afford the Austin-Healey they always wanted. The same will probably hold true in the future. If you want an investment, contact your broker. If you want a car for those beautiful spring days and long summer nights, buy a Healey.

What you're really getting when you buy an Austin-Healey is a car that you can own cost free. All cars cost money to operate—money that's usually lost forever. Gasoline, tires, oil and insurance have never been, and never will be, free. With Healeys the prices are climbing just steadily enough for you to recoup most of these expenses, which is not a bad situation. When people talk about the rising prices of Austin-Healeys this is what they're really saying. Remember, the prices will go up, usually just enough for you to stay even with the maintenance costs and inflation; not enough to replace your money market fund.

The early cars are for the wind-in-the-face crowd, people who don't mind getting wet occasionally. A lot of people still believe these early four-cylinder cars are the only true Austin-Healeys, and they could very well be right. One thing for sure is that the values of these cars will continue to climb. Some of them are approaching a quarter of a century old now and there will never be anything like them again. BN1 and BN2 cars are the real bargains. Get one today; they're never going to be cheaper.

The 100-Six cars are the enigma. They were less car than the four-cylinder ones that came before them, and also less car than the big 3000's that followed. The current prices reflect just that position. These are very nice cars that have been the subject of very bad press. A lot of the opinions about the 100-Six cars have been formed by people who have never driven them.

The truth is that by this time in the model's history a car's *condition* is more important than what it might have been like when new. There are a lot of 3000's that are less desirable than a good 100-Six, just as the reverse is true. You should be more concerned with the condition of the car than the specific type of six-cylinder Healey you want.

If you want features like windows that roll up and down the field is considerably smaller. You're "stuck" with the elegant Healeys, the late model 3000's. These Mark III 3000's, for many, represent the finest hour. The Austin-Healey that was introduced in the early fifties could go no further. Any additional elaboration, or refinement, would have been out of character. The circle was complete.

The next group of cars are the fun ones: the Sprites. The Bugeyes are as popular right now as the MG TD's were ten years ago. If you plot the price curve of the Bugeye you'll find that it is almost a duplicate of the MG T series. The cars came a decade apart but they're so similar in concept that no one should be surprised to be looking at $12,000 Bugeyes. There was a time when you could buy several dozen for that kind of money. Then again, I sold a flawless MG TD for $800 in the early sixties.

The Austin-Healey Sprite story went downhill from the Bugeye, and the current prices reflect that. The more recent Sprites will never reach the same status as the car that everybody thought was so stupid looking in 1960. The Bugeye is an institution; nothing else comes close.

Any Austin-Healey is going to be worth a lot more if it's fully optioned. In the case of the Sprite it's quite easy to simply scrounge around junk yards and come up with wire wheels and disc brakes for the front. These little items not only make the car look better but they may also bring the value up. This will

11

only be the case if you stick to the original factory options. Anything else will bring the value of the car down. The Bugeyes that will appreciate most in the future will be the original cars.

These are points best discussed over beer on Saturday afternoons after the concours judging. There's a lot more agreement about 1275 cc engines in Bugeyes; they're not original, just better. They are also beginning to lower the value, so be careful here. With Bugeyes you have to decide between fun and authenticity.

When you get to the 100M cars you could find a real fraud. These cars are rare enough so that most people have never seen or driven one. That means you won't get to comparison shop when you do find one for sale. The best solution is to read everything you can about the cars and then make the rounds of all the Healey shows. Most larger shows will have at least one example on display and the owner will be more than happy to show you how the car differs from the plain BN2.

When it comes to the 100S you're on your own. These cars bring such high prices that it might be well worth getting someone who knows about Austin-Healeys to help you select one. The time has come when just about any car can be built from extra pieces (just ask someone in England about the number of counterfeit Formula 1 cars running in vintage racing today).

Rust forms in the rear wheel well of Sprites, especially in the part of the panel with the bead. It's a good idea to clean this area very carefully with a wire brush. When all the debris has been removed, paint and then cover it with some type of nonhardening undercoat. Author photo.

There were times when the factory used the hyphen and other times it was left out. This same thing occurs in articles about the cars. At this point it seems that you can simply take your choice. We have gone with the hyphen.

The most obvious problem with Healeys is the one you'll notice first: the rust. Remember, these cars were built well before anyone had any notion of how to construct a car so it wouldn't rust into the ground. On the Healey, anything that touched water on the street seemed to rust, and rust with a vengeance. Also remember that what you see is only part of the problem; do yourself a favor and assume that it will look worse when you poke around the car in the privacy of your own garage.

People who live in dry climates don't really comprehend all of this, but when they spot a Healey from the eastern half of the United States they'll quickly understand the destructive force of rust. And that leads to the caution that just because you locate a Healey in the land of sunshine, don't assume that it never saw the snowbelt. A lot of Healeys spent their early years rusting, only to later find their way to a milder final resting place.

The lower part of the body panels seem to go first, usually the first twelve inches above the ground. This includes such things as the trunk floor, inner body panels, the trunk lid opening and even the gas tank. The frame outriggers and the front cross-member below the radiator also rust badly. The entire lower part of the body will rust from the rear of the front fender well to the rear of the car.

Another place that is attacked by corrosion is the battery storage area. This is located directly behind the seats, as seen on this 100M, and consists of two 6-volt batteries. This arrangement is similar to the system used by the MGA. Unfortunately, most people ignore the area and the battery supports rot away. Author photo.

In very severe cases the frame itself has even been known to rust away. This is usually not a problem in the forward part of the chassis, though, because of the way a Healey leaks oil—it sort of spreads its own rust-proof film all over this part of the chassis.

The other places you'll find rust are in the trunk floor and in the rocker panels. These pieces are available on the replacement market and should cause no major problem, except maybe to your wallet. The thing to remember is that on a Healey, rust is like an iceberg, you can only see the tip of the problem. The bulk of it is underneath.

When it comes to repairing all of these rusted areas you need to consider right away whether or not you'll use fiberglass for replacement. Among real Austin-Healey fanatics using it is heresy. This could make you an "untouchable" at some Healey meets. Besides, most fiberglass fenders don't fit very well. Also, as the car is driven, stress cracks will develop in the panels. The fiberglass simply doesn't respond to all the vibration as well as the original metal panels.

While you'll seldom see rust in the front of the chassis, you could see a bent chassis. The car doesn't even have to have been in a wreck for this to happen. I've seen the frame rails on Healeys that have never been in a crash that look as if someone threw boulders from the depths of Hell at the bottom of the frame. They were simply cases of too many obstacles and too many floor jacks. This is a vulnerable car.

While you're down on your hands and knees, check for crash damage and poor frame straightening. As you view the car from the front the main frame rails should be straight as an arrow all the way to the rear. If they aren't, just walk away from the car—you have discovered an Austin-Healey you do not want.

It is also a very flexible car. When you try to restore a Healey make sure you put the motor in before you replace the body panels. If you carefully install all the panels, and then put the engine in, the panels can pull out of alignment. The weight of the engine will put that much twist into the chassis.

The engines of these cars are no small matter. Six-cylinders are a lot of engine. If you're used to working on Chevrolets you might not mind all of that weight but remember that this block is actually heavier than that of a Chevy. Even the four-cylinder jobs are a lot of steel to be lifted around the garage. Only the Sprite engines can be tossed about on the workbench.

Fortunately, there isn't too much that can go wrong with these engines—except all of the usual things. Most often they seem to burn a lot of oil; what they're not leaking, that is. All Healeys seem to go through valve guides on a regular basis. How the designers managed to engineer this feature into every single Healey from the early four-cylinder cars right through the Sprites is one of the great mysteries. Don't try to understand it, just believe it; and install bronze valve guides as a replacement.

One point to be careful of is that you don't rush into a valve job on one of these cars. I once did the usual "decoke," or valve job, on a Healey that burned only a little oil, and when I got through it burned a whole lot of oil. When the top end was all sealed up, the oil had to go someplace—and it did, right past a set of worn-out piston rings. If you're going to take a motor apart, make sure you do the whole thing. These motors don't respond to partial jobs.

Another item to be careful of, especially on the Austin-Healey Sprites, is rockershaft wear. The oil doesn't seem to reach the shafts and they wear at a phenomenal rate. They are also very expensive. The good part is that Sprite camshafts don't wear out nearly as quickly as the ones on the big cars.

Right behind the engine lies an expensive problem: the transmission. I sometimes believe the British are trying to balance their trade deficit with the exportation of transmission parts. Six-hundred-dollar parts bills are not totally out of the picture on some of these gearboxes. Add in the labor and you can see why a lot of people learn to live with bad gearboxes. If there is a problem here, make sure you can afford it.

The owner of this 100 series Austin-Healey got carried away: Chrome wire wheels look very nice but they can also lose you points at a major concours meet. On a perfect show car every part should have the same finish that it had when it left the Healey factory. Author photo.

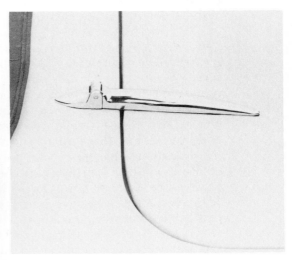

One of the key areas to look at on a car is the quality of the chrome. Chroming is expensive and if you're going to have to spend money at the platers then figure it into the price of the car. Poor-quality plating is just as bad as if the original chrome is rusted. Also, if the brightwork is badly pitted you may have to buy an entirely new part. Author photo.

If there isn't a problem, make sure you don't cause one. Most gearbox problems are inflicted by the driver. Oil levels are allowed to get low, gears are ground and the gearboxes are used to slow the cars to a halt. Downshifting may be fun but remember that the brakes were designed to stop the car. Besides, they are far easier, and cheaper, to replace than gearboxes.

The overdrive, on the other hand, is usually not a major problem. If it doesn't work, check all of the electrical circuits. The problem is most likely with the electrics, not the mechanicals. The process of finding an electrical problem is never easy, just a lot cheaper than finding a mechanical one.

When it comes to the rear axle you shouldn't have any problems—if you leave it alone, that is. Most rear axle problems come from people "fixing" them. The average Saturday mechanic simply cannot handle rear axle work. Leave it alone. If there is a problem find a professional mechanic who knows Healeys.

When it comes to the wheels you can look for problems. I've seen very few Healeys that have five round, and true, wire wheels. The big Austin-Healeys just don't look right with steel disc wheels, no matter how easy they might be to take care of. If you're looking at a Healey with wire wheels figure in the replacement cost of a couple of wire wheels.

Another problem with some Healeys is that people haven't cared for the drive splines. When you remove a wheel, make sure the hub splines are cleaned and covered with grease. When the splines get dirty and are left in wretched condition they wear very quickly. Two things can then happen: The wheel could fall off, or the wheel could be impossible to remove. Since both conditions are serious you should clean the splines and grease them on a regular basis.

While you're down on your hands and knees poking around under the car check the condition of the shock absorbers. These are the old-style lever shocks and they're expensive to replace. Rebuilt shocks are now available, but some of them may be in worse shape than the originals. Pay special attention to the condition of the bushings in the lever arm, as these are often totally worn out. In the rear it's the link that might need replacement. In fact, these worn bushings and links are usually as much of a problem as the shock absorbers.

One area in which you can be sure to have problems is the electrical system; after all, it's a Lucas. Austin-Healey electrical systems weren't all that good when the car was delivered to its original owner. Now, twenty or thirty years later, you should be surprised only if you don't have trouble. The only thing you'll need in order to master this situation is patience. Also, remember to always check the condition of the grounds first. When a car rusts as badly as Healeys do, the ground is the first place to check. There's been a lot written on the subject of Lucas electricals, and most every experienced English car owner considers himself an "expert" on Lucas electrical systems.

When you're looking for a Healey of any model to buy, try to find one with as sound a body as possible. The engine condition is secondary. It's a lot easier, and cheaper, to rebuild engines than it is to do quality bodywork. This is especially true of the big Healeys. And when it comes to Sprites this is even more true, since in this case the body *is* the chassis, that being the nature of unit construction. When the body is rusted, you've got a weak chassis on your hands.

The best way to approach a ground up restoration, here, is to simply strip the car of all its parts and send the chassis to the metal stripper. When it returns you can begin the process of patching the rust holes. Since these body panels are actually stressed members, you should weld in the new pieces, not just use fiberglass and putty.

The Jensen-Healey presents still a different set of problems. This model has a tremendous amount of plastic trim and rubber hoses. Very few people are currently performing ground up restorations on these cars so the best thing to do is locate the best example you can find and take very good care of it.

Assuming that your quest for the perfect Healey has ended and the money and title have changed hands, you're now ready for the drive home. The most exciting part is what you'll

Poorly aligned panels will also cost you points at a major meet. This simply reinforces the old story that going from a 98-point show car to one that will get 100 points doubles the price of the restoration. Author photo.

actually learn about the car on this trip. If you have to tow the car home, or it comes home as boxes of parts, you're on your own. Buying a basket case puts you in a special category of ambitiously wise man, or fool—the truth being known only months down the road, when you finally determine, within several thousand dollars, how much it'll cost to get the turkey on the road.

After your neighbors have looked the car over and stopped asking, "You paid *how* much?" you're ready for the first work on the new car. Forget about the new interior and stay with the basics, things like lube jobs and oil changes. A lot of people like to take their new possession down to the car wash and blow all the grease off the underside of the engine compartment and chassis. The only problem is that on a Healey this grease coating keeps one more place from rusting; remove it and you have a new place for rust to form.

The first thing you might do is give the car a basic tune-up—nothing fancy, just your average plugs-and-points tune-up. You can use a manual such as those put out by Haynes or Bentley as a guide. First, examine the old spark plugs as you remove them. They'll tell you a lot about the condition of the engine, as will a compression check, something you might as well do as long as the plugs are out. You might also need to replace the plug wires. If they appear cracked and dried out just replace them, don't ask questions.

Adjusting the valves and carbs is not as difficult as it first appears, unless you've purchased the three-carburetor 3000. Just follow the manual very closely and don't rush. Also, either clean or replace the air cleaners. If your car has the wire mesh type, soak them in kerosene overnight and then brush them clean. Lightly oil them before you bolt them back on the carbs.

While you're under the hood, check the condition of the fan belts and water pump, all the while looking for leaks in the cooling system. Just to be on the safe side you might want to replace the coolant, flushing the system before adding new antifreeze. Since the cooling system has always seemed marginal on Healeys this is an important area to keep in excellent condition. If your cooling system is at all questionable remove the radiator and have it renovated by a radiator shop. Money spent here is good insurance.

Now that you've performed all of your little miracles under the hood it's time to take your new prize for another drive. Your Healey should run a little better now, or a lot better, depending on what you bought with all the money pilfered from your grocery budget. Watch your gauges carefully and note what they all read. When the car is fully warmed up, head back home and get ready to change the oil.

While the oil is draining into the pan you can amuse yourself by looking for oil leaks. You'll find them. There may well be an English motor that doesn't leak oil but I haven't seen it yet. After using all kinds of exotic gasket sealers I've finally decided the only way to prevent oil leaks would be to simply weld the engine together!

When you replace the oil use a quality brand. There is no reason to ever be cheap about oil. The results of using cheap oil will be even more expensive than the quality oil would have cost. The same goes for the filter: Use a quality oil filter.

Now the time has come for a grease job. An Austin-Healey has more lube fittings than five modern cars. You want to make sure that you hit every one of them. Just follow the manual and make sure everything is well greased, and remember no one ever said owning an Austin-Healey would be easy. The lube chart includes parts like the door hinge pins, hood latches and even the rear springs. Do all of them.

By this time the end of the day is arriving and you'll want to take the car for another drive. This is all well and good. Just keep in mind that there are a number of other things that will need attending to the next day (for example, the transmission and rear axle oil). Also, the brakes should be bled until you've removed most of the old fluid. Use Castrol fluid, not an American brand. And put a light coating of grease on the wheel hub splines before you replace the wire wheels.

Gauges can be rebuilt with new innerworkings and refinished faces. The mileage can also be reset at the same time (not a good idea). It's a lot cheaper to have your instruments rebuilt than to purchase new ones. The steering wheel in this BN1 is original. Author photo.

By the time you finish all of this you'll know more about your Austin-Healey than the last two owners combined. You'll also have an idea of what it'll take to keep the thing running. The thing to remember about these cars is that when you replace something, try to keep the car original, which in many cases will mean *returning* it to original. Austin-Healeys will never be this cheap again, and the cars that will go highest in value will be those that are closest to factory original. The correct part may well be a little more expensive than one that's close, but don't be tempted. Keep bringing the car closer to the way it was when it left the factory. You and your bank account will be happier when the day arrives for a new owner.

No matter what Austin-Healey you're looking at, your first step should be to join the local Austin-Healey club. These people will know your car better than you do and several people will most likely have owned the model you want, or will be thinking of buying one.

Somehow I just can't imagine "Nissan of Japan" on the fender of a car. English cars are unique, they have class and distinction. Even the emblems are elegant. The problem was that the English couldn't keep up the effort. The world passed them by, which is exactly why all of us restore them today. It's a way of going back to a different era.

This is what Austin-Healeys are all about—relaxing. Restoring your Austin-Healey is something you do in your spare time. The reason is that you want to just sit around and enjoy it on those nice summer days.

This is another example of the perfectly restored Healey. The owner didn't restore the original sidecurtains to keep out the rain; he did it to have a perfectly restored car. Chances are the top and sidecurtains have never seen a single raindrop.

INVESTMENT RATING

One of the features of this series of books is an investment rating for each of the various models available to collectors. Very few people have ever invested in an Austin-Healey; they simply enjoy them. The system below outlines each of the five categories that several hundred Healey owners would use in rating Austin-Healeys.

★★★★★ The best investments. Already fairly expensive, but continued appreciation can be expected. The best examples of these cars are usually well known and are often sold between Austin-Healey collectors without any advertising.

★★★★ Excellent cars to own. More affordable than the five-star Austin-Healeys, but still not cheap. These are almost the best but not quite as prized as the cars in the higher category.

★★★ Good value. These Austin-Healeys are less expensive than the four- and five-star cars. They will also appreciate less. These are generally solid cars with good qualities and offer a lot of driving enjoyment. They may not go very high in price but they give a lot of fun for the money. A good buy for the first-time Austin-Healey buyer.

★★ Good Austin-Healeys to buy and enjoy. They may not have all the traditional characteristics but they are still fun to own and drive. Just don't look for much appreciation. The best they will do is to hold their value.

★ Any Austin-Healey with lots of rust and a burned-out engine. Also, those Austin-Healeys that it makes no sense at all to restore. These cars will cost more money to put in merely presentable shape than the car would ever be worth.

CHAPTER 1
100, SERIES BN1

SERIAL NUMBERS
133237-228046

There was nothing new about the idea. Donald Healey had been using it for years. Take some parts from a production car, put them together in a new way and watch the people line up to buy them. The big difference this time around was that the lines became gigantic, especially in the United States.

Donald Healey had been to the United States enough times to know that there would be a sizable market for an open two-seater car that was fast and stylish. This was no tremendous insight, since the folks over at Standard-Triumph had arrived at exactly the same conclusion, and were busy getting the TR2 into production at the same time Donald Healey was moving ahead.

The Austin-Healey would be different from the Triumph but not so much so as to put the car in a totally different market. The Triumph and Austin-Healey began as rivals; and when there's only one model of each marque left, each owner will probably denigrate the other's car.

The BN1 is one of those cars that just screams sports car, from the fold-down windshield to the narrow wire wheels. The car was an instant success in the market. In the first year Healey was turning out 100 cars a week—an impressive number, since previous Healey efforts hadn't produced a total of a thousand cars.

If you're looking for one of these cars to purchase you may want to get involved in the serial number game. This is something that hasn't really had an effect on the prices of early Austin-Healeys yet but, based on other cars, it will. The early numbers always seem to bring higher prices and, in the case of these first Austin-Healeys, there is the advantage of having alloy body panels. These make the car not only faster, but rarer. If you're really concerned about getting a collector car then try to find one of the cars with the alloy body panels. The steel hood was introduced at Body Number 3397 and the steel trunk lid was introduced at Body Number 3129. When the rest of the alloy panels were changed to steel is still the subject of speculation.

The best part of these early Healeys is the fold-down windshields. On this car you can once again see the attention to detail. One of the problems with buying a basket case, or a car you bring home in cardboard boxes, is that a lot of these little parts will be missing. Replacing them will be an expensive and time-consuming project. Author photo.

This is it: the very first Austin-Healey prototype. The headlights are lower than those of the production cars but the rest remained the same. Jaguar Cars, Inc., photo.

When BMC (British Motor Corporation) decided to take on the Austin-Healey production there was no way the Tickford works could supply the necessary bodies, at least not in the quantity needed. Before production moved to Longbridge, though, Donald Healey assembled twenty cars at Warwick, with the bodies supplied by Jensen. In the cars that followed these, the fenders were made of steel; the beginning of a major rust problem.

While on the subject of Austin-Healey bodies, it should be mentioned that they have one item that no other mass production car has. Each body panel and major trim piece has the serial number stamped on it. If you want to check on whether or not the Healey you're looking at has been damaged or altered from the original in any way, check to see if the numbers all match with the tag in the engine compartment. In the long run the cars with matching numbers will be the most valuable. If nothing else, matching numbers are an indication that the car has never been in a serious crash.

The BN1 may still be one of the finest collector cars around. It looks as good as, if not better than, it did on the day of its introduction. There are a lot of these early cars around, but not so many that you'll see yourself coming and going. The major problem you'll have with a BN1 is the problem you'll have with any Austin-Healey: rust.

The body parts of a Healey are large and expensive. Even more importantly, they are largely unavailable. Because the Healey body panels are so large, the amount of money it would take to create a stamping die for them is even larger. The best substitutes for new fenders are the patch panels that are available from places like Moss Motors. These are welded into place after the rusted sections are removed. Some Austin-Healey suppliers have the full panels available; but remember the importance of serial numbers on the panels.

One thing that you should find on all BN1 Healeys, besides the rust, is an overdrive. Three-speed transmissions were hardly exciting, even then, and the speed of the Healey was hardly phenomenal; thus, the overdrive was made standard. The result was really a five-speed gearbox, which, in conjunction with the 4.12:1 rear axle gearing, did rather nicely.

When shopping for one of these early cars, your major questions should be: "Is it all here? Am I buying a whole car? What parts are missing or damaged? What makes this car a BN1?" The first thing to look for is the three-speed gearbox. Next, make sure the side crease does not continue beyond the rear wheel. Another quick check is that on the BN1's the overdrive switch is on the dash panel, not on the smaller instrument pod.

If all three of these items match up, then you're looking at a BN1. The next step is to compare the serial number on the

Here is the engine that set the legend. It had 2660 cc when the MG was getting along with less than 1500 cc and the TR2 had less than two liters. This engine is an example of the kind you'll find in the best of the show cars. Note the absence of chrome where none originally existed, and the tremendous attention to detail. This is the kind of car you can expect to pay top dollar for. Author photo.

edge of the hood stamping with the chassis number. It should be the same in both places, at least on a totally original car. Then make sure that the chassis number is lower than 228047. If all of this matches, bet the ranch and dog that you're looking at a BN1.

There are very few, if any, attempts to sell a BN1 as a BN2, or vice versa. There isn't enough price difference to make it worthwhile. If it happens, it's done through ignorance. Only when the transaction involves 100M's and 100S's is serious fraud involved. With a BN1 or BN2 you just want to protect yourself against an ignorant seller.

If you've determined that you are indeed looking at a correct car, start checking its condition. The first stop is the motor. The biggest problem here is overheating—Healeys are legendary in this department. The real danger is that you might have a blown head gasket or, worse yet, a warped or even cracked cylinder head. It may very well be the case that the head has been shaved several times during the last quarter of a century, in which case you could have a real problem, since there would be nothing left to take off.

Another difficulty could be the timing chain. The biggest problem here is usually the rubber tensioner ring. This ring, like all rubber parts, begins to deteriorate and falls to the bottom of the sump. Then the whole assembly begins to go south. This isn't a major item, just something to take notice of, and to figure into the cost of putting the car right.

The rest of the engine and transmission are no different from any other engine that's seen a lot of miles. Some of the parts are not available new, which would mean a search for decent used parts. The shift rails are now once again available, and they may as well be replaced when you open the box. The thing to keep in mind is that this gearbox is different from that of every other Austin-Healey on the road.

The same goes for the rear axle. This is a sturdy piece of equipment and shouldn't have any real problems unless the previous owner had a fondness for "stop light Gran Prix" races. If the baulk rings in the transmission are worn out, start looking for a used gearbox. These rings are pressed onto the gears themselves, and it's actually easier to find better gears than to make the repairs. One thing to check is the area around the wheel studs. The cast hub is very prone to cracking where the stud is pressed into the assembly.

When it comes to the suspension, the entire mechanism is straightforward, early British engineering. The lever shocks may be covered in hydraulic fluid, in which case you can rest assured they will need to be rebuilt. Rebuild kits are available, as are completely rebuilt units. The prices of either are very rea-

The BN1's have the smoothest rear contours of all the early Austin-Healeys. The fender reflectors were not yet a part of the car. Don't try to identify a car by parts not present, though, since many owners have incorporated wrong parts onto the cars over the years. Author photo.

Some BN1's came with this reflector installed. All cars manufactured after October 25, 1954, had to have rear reflectors. Author photo.

Another easy way to tell a BN1 from a BN2 is to look at the gearshift lever. If it has three speeds it's probably a BN1, if it has four forward speeds it's either a BN2 or a BN1 with a transplant. Author photo.

sonable. The springs of the early cars, however, won't interchange with anything on the later cars; the spring rates are different, even if the size is not.

The final point to check is the frame. It has usually led a hard life. In the front of the frame you should look for crash damage; both the usual kind from an accident and the kind that Austin-Healeys get from running over road obstacles. (No one ever said there was decent road clearance in a Healey.) In the rear, and along the sides, look for rust.

The other thing to remember about these early Healeys is that they are not for everyone, just as they are not for everyday transportation. It's a good idea to think of the big Austin-Healeys as being on a continuum. On one end are the early 100's and on the other end are the later 3000's—a pure sports car on one end and a touring car on the other.

If you want pure, postwar classic motoring then the early cars are for you. If you prefer creature comforts, like windows that roll up and down, and consoles on the driveshaft tunnel, it's best to stick to the later 3000's.

The BN1's have been climbing in price recently, and they should continue to appreciate faster than the other production Healeys. They provide everything that could be desired in an English sports car. They may not be everybody's idea of comfort, but they are fun.

100 BN1

ENGINE
TYPE: 4-cylinder
BORE X STROKE: mm/inches: 87.3X111.1/ 3.438X4.375
DISPLACEMENT: cc/cubic inches: 2660/ 162.2
VALVE OPERATION: ohv, pushrod operation
COMPRESSION RATIO: 7.5:1
CARBURETION: 2 SU H4 1½"
BHP: 90 bhp @ 4000 rpm
CHASSIS & DRIVETRAIN
TRANSMISSION: 3-speed, overdrive on 2nd and 3rd gears
FRONT SUSPENSION: independent, coil springs, lever arm dampers

REAR SUSPENSION: live axle, half elliptic springs, lever shocks
AXLE RATIO: 4.125:1 spiral bevel
GENERAL
OVERALL LENGTH: 12'7"
WHEELBASE: 7'6"
TRACK, front: 4'1"
rear: 4'2.75"
BRAKES, front: drums, 11X1¾"
rear: drums, 11X1¾"
TIRE SIZE: 5.90X15
WHEEL SIZE: 4.5X15
WEIGHT: 2,176 lbs. for original cars
PERFORMANCE
ACCELERATION: 0-30: 3.3 seconds, 0-60: 10.3 seconds
TOP SPEED: 111 mph

This is the dash on a BN1. The overdrive switch is on the dash panel proper and the ignition switch is on the instrument panel. The BN2 cars use opposite positions. Author photo.

When buying an early Healey keep in mind that you're buying a collector car. That means that as many of the original parts should be present as possible. Even though very few people ever drive a Healey with the top up and the side curtains in place, they should be a part of the car. The more parts that are missing the lower your offer should be. Author photo.

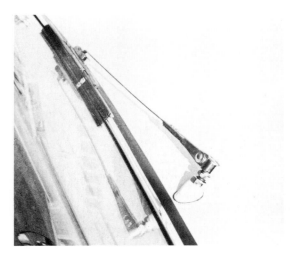

Still another way to tell a BN1 from a BN2: On the first series the windshield wiper bezels should be painted. On the BN2 they should be chrome. Author photo.

The tops on these early Healeys only seem to go up for the shows. It's hard to imagine anyone driving with one erect. First, the side vision is none too great. Second, the wind in your face is what it's all about! Author photo.

This is a full dash of the BN1. The steering wheel is original, as is everything else on the dash. Author photo.

Too often people attending vintage sports car races assume they're viewing an exact representation of what happened in the fifties. Here is one of the earliest Austin-Healey racers. The car is a BN1 driven by Dick Stockton at Stockton Air Base in 1956. Petit-pierre photo.

SERIAL NUMBERS
228047-233455

The BN2 is the one with the real four-speed. Granted, you can get four gears out of a BN1 by removing a little plate but this Austin-Healey has four real gears forward—not three forward speeds and a first gear for pulling stumps.

Looking at the gearshift knob is really the quickest way to tell the BN1 and BN2 apart. The rest of the car is so similar that at fifty feet only the most dedicated Healey fan can tell the difference.

One difference between the models that is apparent from the side view is the front wheel cutouts. The arches on the BN2 are slightly larger, although you must be careful of the BN1 that has had BN2 fenders attached somewhere along the line. And just to make it even more fun, some early BN2's had BN1 fenders attached at the factory!

The other way to tell the difference is by the placement of the overdrive switch. In the BN2 it is always to the right of the steering wheel; whereas on the earlier cars it was simply placed on the dash panel, not on the instrument cluster panel.

Unless you have a real passion for a BN1, the BN2 is the best car for the early Healey fan. Along with the gearbox, the brakes were improved as well. While the designers were at it, the rear axle was also improved, or rather replaced with one from a Morris design.

The BN2 is a better purchase than the BN1, since the improvements make it a better car. There doesn't seem to be any difference in price between the two cars, so this is the better buy. Also, there were less than 4,000 BN2's built (as opposed to over 10,000 BN1's). They were only produced for a year, which makes them rare compared to the BN1 cars, but doesn't make them more collectible.

The BN2 was around for such a short time that very few magazines got around to testing one. Only when *Autocar* editors got a chance to visit the RSAC's Scottish Rally in 1956 did they test one. They found the four-speed gearbox, with overdrive, to be quite pleasant. They also found the trunk to be rather large and easy to use when they packed for the trip.

This is the BN2, the second rarest of all the production Healeys, and also an improved car over the BN1. This particular car is one of the later BN2's, since it carries the side crease through to the panel behind the rear wheel. Also, the wheel cutouts in the fenders are different from the BN1 model. Author photo.

One of the key recognition points of the BN2 is the larger front wheel cut-out on the fender. The twin wing mirrors were a standard accessory of the period. Author photo.

They thought cruising at eighty miles an hour was rather easy. Try that today and you may get a ticket quicker than you damage the car. Even the heater worked nicely. The most interesting thing about their description of the trip is that if someone today did a similar trip he would probably get a long-distance award from some Austin-Healey club.

Everything the editors of *Autocar* liked in 1956 makes the car equally appealing today. There is no reason these cars have to be trailered from place to place. If they could at one time cruise at eighty, why then can't they be driven today at sixty? People have forgotten just what a nice road car the 100 really is, and for this kind of use the BN2 is the best.

The BN2 is a classic case of when buying the second series of a car makes the most sense for people who intend to use their cars for driving fun. The improvements made in this second series make driving them more enjoyable. In fact they are an all-around better deal for everyone except the collector. The only problem is that there aren't very many of them to choose from.

---

100 BN2

ENGINE
TYPE: 4-cylinder
BORE X STROKE: mm/inches: 87.3X111.1/ 3.438X4.375
DISPLACEMENT: cc/cubic inches: 2660/ 162.2
VALVE OPERATION: ohv, pushrod operation
COMPRESSION RATIO: 7.5:1
CARBURETION: 2 SU H4 1½"
BHP (mfr): 90 bhp @ 4000 rpm
CHASSIS & DRIVETRAIN
TRANSMISSION: 4-speed, overdrive on 3rd and 4th gears
FRONT SUSPENSION: ind., coil springs, lever arm dampers

REAR SUSPENSION: live axle, half elliptic springs, lever shocks
AXLE RATIO: 4.10:1 hypoid drive
GENERAL
OVERALL LENGTH: 12'7"
WHEELBASE: 7'6"
TRACK, front: 4'1"
    rear: 4'2.75"
BRAKES, front: drums, 11X2¼"
    rear: drums, 11X1¾"
TIRE SIZE: 5.90X15
WHEEL SIZE: 4.5X15
WEIGHT: 2,015 lbs.
PERFORMANCE
ACCELERATION: 0-30: 3.3 seconds, 0-60: 10.3 seconds
TOP SPEED: 111 mph

One of the nicest little parts on the 100 series Healeys is the latch for the top. It's a very simple overcenter affair. It looks good, and best of all it works very well. Author photo.

The correct wire wheel is the forty-eight-spoke variety as shown on this car. Wire wheels were standard on the 100-4 series, although over the years a lot of different wire wheels have been substituted for the originals. Austin-Healey never offered chromed wire wheels as an option. They could, though, be ordered as a special option if you had the right connections and could wait for your car. The point is that more cars have chrome wheels today than were ever delivered that way. Author photo.

The reflectors on the rear are generally found on 1954 and 1955 BN2's. Over the years so many things have been taken on and off these early cars, finding out what is correct is a major undertaking. You shouldn't avoid a car simply because a few things don't appear correct. Just negotiate the price in relationship to the condition. Author photo.

The compression ratio on these cars was a mild 7.5:1, which makes them perfect for today's low-quality gasoline. The carburetors on this car are twin H6's, which are a 100M modification. Author photo.

These are the original side curtains. It's amazing what all of us put up with in order to drive sports cars in the fifties! Sliding Plexiglas panels were never made available on the 100 series. Author photo.

This rocker arm cover is a seldom-seen period accessory. These engines put out 94 bhp at 4000 rpm. Author photo.

This is a view of the folding windshield mechanism that was used on the 100 series. All of the English cars of this period used some marvelous machine work. The thumb screw is a beautiful piece of craftsmanship. Author photo.

This photo shows the correct braided hose for the heater, as well as the correct braided wiring harness for the ignition system. It's details like these that add to a car's value. When purchasing one of the early cars, you're buying a collector car, not an everyday driver. The price will depend on how accurate the restoration is. Author photo.

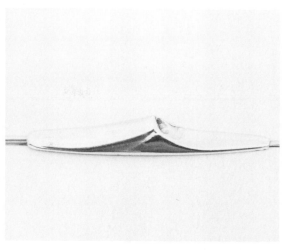

The socket that rests on the front fender exhibits the same sort of craftsmanship. And with the windscreen lowered you can see how these pieces work together. Author photo.

Still another white BN2. This time the front of the car is totally undecorated with accessories. The lack of accessories shows off the beauty of the original Healey design. Author photo.

CHAPTER 3
100S

SERIAL NUMBERS
AHS 3501 to 3510
AHS 3601 to 3610
AHS 3701 to 3710
AHS 3801 to 3810
AHS 3901 to 3910
Works racing cars carried an SPL prefix
SPL 224/226/256/257/258

This is it. Finding a 100S is like finding the perfect spouse. It takes a long time and it isn't cheap but it's well worth the effort. The 100S costs a lot of money to buy today but it will cost even more next year. The 100S is the King of the Healey Hill.

They weren't even called 100S until after the 1954 Sebring event. They were just plain BN2's—a little improved, maybe, but no special names. The S was for Sebring, and that was meant to play to the American market. Geoffrey Healey (Donald's son) wrote in *Austin Healey: The Story of the Big Healeys* that the car was designed for the American dealers who wanted something that would carry the racing banner, and sell more cars. This was an early version of the "Win on Sunday, sell on Monday" philosophy.

The basis for the car was the standard 100 body shell and chassis. John Thompson, the Healey chassis builder, took the Standard frames and made them a little stronger by welding some extra gussets and the like in place. In an effort to keep the weight down, aluminum was substituted for steel wherever possible.

Then some extra-large shock brackets were installed before the whole unit was shipped over to Jensen to have the aluminum body installed. None of the original 100S cars had provisions for tops or side windows, but often these luxuries have been added along the way.

The engines were fabricated by the folks in the Austin shop. The cylinder head was cast in aluminum and the manifold was attached in such a way that the carbs were vertical, not the usual angle. These cylinder heads, designed by Weslake, were totally different from the standard Austin head. The heads proved to be rather fragile so make sure the one on your car is authentic. For what you're going to pay for a 100S you should make every effort to ensure that it comes with all the right parts.

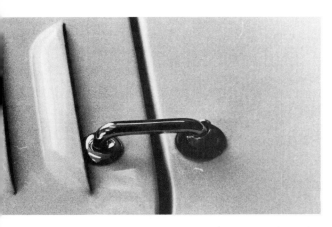

A lot of the little items on rare cars such as the 100S are simply not available as reproductions. This front hood clip is an example. Either it comes with the car or else the new owner faces an expensive project to obtain a new one. Author photo.

This is the rarest and most desirable Austin-Healey. Only 55 were ever produced and 37 of the cars can be accounted for today. Almost all the cars were painted in this blue and white scheme. BMC photo.

The transmissions in these cars were the same as those used in the BN2's. The overdrive was not offered, since it wasn't really necessary and, besides, it would just add weight.

The 100S was one of the first cars to use disc brakes on all four wheels. The 100S was also the first and only production Healey to be so equipped. They aren't quite as good as what we're used to today, but for their day they were unbeatable. They're a nightmare if you have to change brake pads but most of today's owners really don't drive the cars all that much (a pity, really).

The 100S was equipped with a twenty-gallon fuel tank with the filler neck sticking right up through the rear panel behind the cockpit. Everything about this car said *racer*. Even the paint, white with a blue side inset, was carried out to show American racing colors.

Just in case you might not believe the car was fast, *Autocar* found it could easily do eighty in second gear, with the four-speed box yet. The car was still running strong at 110 mph when the testers had to back down. They found the car to be comfortable and nicely balanced and they could easily put the car into a four-wheel drift.

The really good part about owning one of these cars is that the basic chassis, inner body panels and suspension are all standard BN2. The engine and brake parts are the only items that are really hard to find. The four-speed gearbox is a closer ratio than a normal BN2, and the rear axle is the spiral bevel found on later cars.

Easy access to the parts also means that counterfeiting of the cars, if not easy, is at least possible. Since only fifty-five of the cars were made, their rarity has shot prices into the stratosphere. More exactly, the price is now at the point where counterfeiters can make a nice profit. Be careful.

Also be careful of anyone selling factory team cars. They are especially rare. This is one Healey you must be prepared to do a lot of homework on before you leave your money with someone. If you already own one it's like having your own personal bank. Even better than that, you can drive it on nice days.

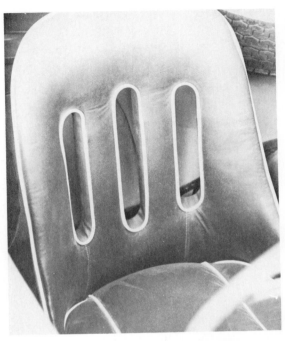

One of the most beautiful items on the 100S is the gas cap. It was manufactured out of aluminum and resided directly in the middle of the back panel behind the cockpit. Author photo.

The seats, like so many parts of the car, are unique to the 100S. No other Austin-Healey had the cooling slots in the backrest. They were all finished in blue leather with white piping. Author photo.

The cap was connected to the massive fuel tank which held 20 Imperial gallons (36 American). The fuel lines were all 3/8 inch in diameter. Notice that the fuel tank had a gauge, something seldom seen on modern racing cars. Author photo.

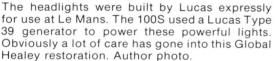

The headlights were built by Lucas expressly for use at Le Mans. The 100S used a Lucas Type 39 generator to power these powerful lights. Obviously a lot of care has gone into this Global Healey restoration. Author photo.

Only a single taillight was used at the rear, and no reflector. Bumpers were another thing the 100S lacked. It had the most graceful lines of all the Austin-Healeys. Author photo.

100S AHS

ENGINE
TYPE: 4-cylinder, the same as the BN1, but with an aluminum cylinder head containing separate ports for each intake and exhaust valve

BORE X STROKE: mm/inches: 87.3X111.1/ 3.438X4.375

DISPLACEMENT: cc/cubic inches: 2660/ 162.2

VALVE OPERATION: ohv, pushrod operation

COMPRESSION RATIO: 8.3:1

CARBURETION: 2 SU H6 1¾"

BHP (mfr): 132 bhp @ 4700 rpm

CHASSIS & DRIVETRAIN
TRANSMISSION: 4-speed, no overdrive

FRONT SUSPENSION: ind., coil springs, lever arm dampers

REAR SUSPENSION: live axle, half elliptic springs, lever shocks

AXLE RATIO: 2.92:1

GENERAL
OVERALL LENGTH: 12'4"

WHEELBASE: 7'6"

TRACK, front: 4'1.6"
        rear: 4'2.75"

BRAKES, front: discs, 11.5"
        rear: discs, 11.5"

TIRE SIZE: 5.50X15 racing tires

WHEEL SIZE: 4.5X15

WEIGHT: 1,924 lbs.

PERFORMANCE
ACCELERATION: 0-30: 3.2 seconds, 0-60: 7.8 seconds

TOP SPEED: 126 mph

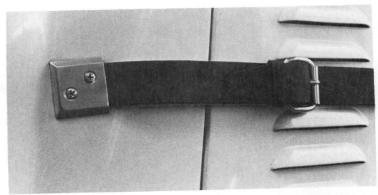

Just to make sure that the hood stayed in place, a leather belt was installed over the hood. This feature was also carried over to the 100M. Note that the correct leather strap has no lamb's wool backing, a feature that too many show cars have. Author photo.

The body was constructed of all-alloy panels, as were all the structural members. The windscreen runs the full width of the cockpit and provides only the minimal frontal area. No provision was made for side curtains or a top. Since the parts from a BN1 would fit, a few owners installed them on the 100S if they used it as a road car. Author photo.

The cylinder head is an aluminum casting. The head was modified from the early type of cylinder and the carburetors mounted on a vertical plane, rather than on an angle. The intake valves are 1.813 inches in diameter as opposed to a standard 1.725. The exhausts went from a normal 1.415 to 1.625 inches in diameter. The motor produced 132 bhp at 4700 rpm. The compression ratio was a relatively low 8.3:1. Author photo.

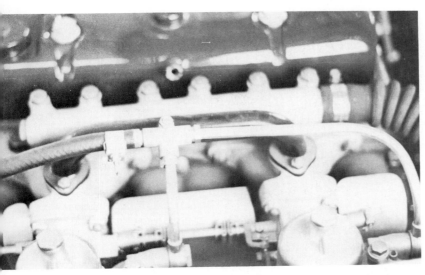

The interesting point here is that cooling water is taken out at
three different locations to improve cooling, always a weak point
with aluminum cylinder heads. The carburetors are 1¾ HD6 SU's.
The fuel was delivered by twin SU LCS pumps. Author photo.

The spare tire found a new location in the 100S. The cars all used
Dunlop racing tires. The steering wheel on this car is not original
but rather is typical of the wooden steering wheels of the period.
Author photo.

The front suspension was independent with wishbones and coil springs, the arms of the upper wishbone being attached to the Armstrong RXP shocks. The round hole in the upper part of the picture is where air ducting for the cockpit was originally installed. Author photo.

This was the only production Austin-Healey ever to have disc brakes on all four wheels. These were built by Dunlop with 11½-inch discs and Mintex pads of 2¼ inches. The discs themselves were hard-chromed for longer life. With no servo assistance the drivers had to have strong legs. The proportioning problem was handled by using calipers with different-sized passages. Author photo.

The front of the car was redesigned from the standard Austin-Healey 100 by Gerry Coker. All of the panels are aluminum. The Austin-Healey badge above the grille is correct. Missing is the 100S badge that mounts on the grille. This is visible, just barely, on the picture of the 100S at racing speed. Author photo.

CHAPTER 4
100M

SERIAL NUMBERS
There are no separate chassis numbers for this series

The 100M is one of the finest Austin-Healeys for the average person to own. Most people have given up on owning a 100S; it's just too rare and too expensive for the average person. Their lust is now focused on the 100M. It may not be cheap to own but it is still possible to put one in your very own garage.

By 1955, people had decided that a little more power was needed for their Healeys. Donald Healey and company decided to oblige the customer by offering a car modified along the lines of the 1953 Le Mans car.

A lot of confusion exists about the Le Mans version of the Austin-Healey, mainly because it really wasn't a separate model. It was a kit installed by the factory on a standard BN2. In fact, roughly one third of the BN2 cars had this kit installed.

This package consisted of two 1¾-inch SU H6 carburetors fitted to a larger intake manifold and, in some cases, a duplicate of the Le Mans camshaft. There was also a cold air box for attaching to the carbs along with a lot of flexible tubing to duct fresh air for improved breathing. Just to make sure the spark occurred at the right time a new distributor with a different advance curve was included. The rest of the kit consisted of a new cylinder head gasket and some stronger valve springs.

In some of the factory cars, as well as some of the kits, a different cam and pistons were included. The factory-quoted figure was 110 bhp at 4500 rpm, instead of 90 bhp at 4000 rpm. The transmission was the same as supplied on the 100S, except an overdrive was added. It was also the same as every other BN2 gearbox.

The suspension was beefed up through the use of a larger front sway bar and stiffer shock absorbers. When *Road & Track* tested the car in 1956 they found the ride a little firmer than the normal 100. They didn't really find it all that appealing but admitted that "the 100M suspension is better suited for competition."

Externally the changes consisted of a louvered hood with a big leather strap holding it down. Also, a different badge, with

Although its hard to see on this black car, the crease on the rear fender is not present. Only the later BN2's had this crease, which is very similar to the 100-Six. Obvious in this photo are the drum brakes that were standard all the way around. Only the 100S got disc brakes. Author photo.

an M on the 100 flash, was installed on the grille. The paint was sometimes a two-tone scheme, similar to, but not exactly the same as, the later cars. This whole kit was available for only $290 over the price of a standard BN2—easily the deal of the decade.

Now comes the difficult part: 100M's came directly from the factory, or most of them did. A truck full of BN2's would be pulled from the assembly line at Longbridge and transported over to Warwick. There the service department would convert them to 100M specifications.

There were also some kits available for dealers to install for customers who wanted to improve their car's performance. These tuning kits were available for the BN1 and continued to be offered at the same time the BN2 was being produced.

This means that all of the engine parts could be installed on the 100 series cars at any time. Graham Robson wrote in *The Big Healeys* that it seemed that not all of the factory cars had all of the pieces installed. Even Geoffrey Healey talks about special pistons, but never mentions how many cars got these fancy pistons, which is an obviously confusing situation.

The important thing today is to make sure that you're buying one of the 1,159 cars that were converted by the factory. The home conversions are very nice and served their purpose in 1955; they made the cars go faster and handle better, but they really aren't prime collector cars. There are several places to check for confirmation as to whether or not the car you're looking at is an authentic 100M.

One of the easiest ways to check is to first make sure that the louvers in the hood are the correct size and style. If these are correct then look for the serial number on the edge of the hood pressing. This number should match the chassis number. If they don't match then you probably have a standard BN2 with a 100M hood.

Next, under the hood on the left side, by the front carburetor, there should be a notch in the inner body upright support. This was put there by the Warwick factory to clear the cold air box. If the notch is in place then you have a 100M: one that was converted at the Warwick works.

The rarest item of all is the 100M grille flash. This may well have been lost long ago, and since no reproductions have been manufactured, don't use it as the sole criteria. If the car has this grille flash, then it's most likely a 100M. Just make sure it has all of the other things as well.

This is the most rapidly appreciating car in the Austin-Healey line, the 100S excepted, so make sure you're getting the real thing. If you do, expect to pay for it. The days when the 100M cost the same as any other BN2 are long gone.

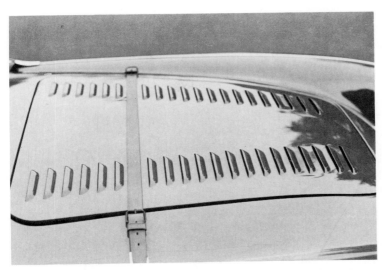

One way to tell if the car is a real 100M is to count, and measure, the louvers on the hood. Next, find the serial number on the hood and see if it matches the commission number on the chassis plate. If those numbers match then the car has passed the test. Author photo.

Here's an example of louvers that are nonoriginal. What they do very well is cool off the driving compartment. It was a very common modification to the early Austin-Healeys. Author photo.

This interior shot shows how the ignition and overdrive switch changed places in the BN2. The dash plaque was placed there by the dealer who imported the car into the United States. The steering wheel is not original but rather a period accessory. Author photo.

100M BN2

ENGINE
TYPE: 4-cylinder
BORE X STROKE: mm/inches: 87.3X111.1/ 3.438X4.375
DISPLACEMENT: cc/cubic inches: 2660/ 162.2
VALVE OPERATION: ohv, pushrod operation
COMPRESSION RATIO: 8.1:1
CARBURETION: 2 SU H6 1¾"
BHP (mfr): 110 bhp @ 4500 rpm

CHASSIS & DRIVETRAIN
TRANSMISSION: 4-speed, overdrive on 3rd and 4th
FRONT SUSPENSION: ind., coil springs, lever arm damper
REAR SUSPENSION: live axle, half elliptic springs, lever shocks

AXLE RATIO: 4.125:1

GENERAL
OVERALL LENGTH: 12'7"
WHEELBASE: 7'6"
TRACK, front: 4'1"
      rear: 4'2.75"
BRAKES, front: drums, 11X2¼"
       rear: drums 11X1¾"
TIRE SIZE: 5.90X15
WHEEL SIZE: 4.5X15
WEIGHT: 2,168 lbs.

PERFORMANCE
ACCELERATION: 0-30: 3.3 seconds, 0-60: 10.0 seconds
TOP SPEED: 118 mph

One of the other special goodies is the cold air box with the little plate stating "This car has been fitted with a LeMans modification Kit." These plates are now being reproduced, so don't use them as a test of authenticity. Author photo.

The ducting that runs from the front of the cold air box to the front of the car is clearly visible in this photo. This car is currently undergoing restoration and offers many interesting items that can only be viewed with the body panels removed. The piece running vertically and located directly in front of the windshield is prone to rust. If an Austin-Healey has rusted rocker panels the rust will probably continue up this support. Fortunately, replacement patch panels are available. Author photo.

This view shows not only the carburetor ducting but the passenger air intake as well. On the right-hand side in the forward edge of the driver's footwell is asbestos. If your feet fry every time you drive your Austin-Healey you might check to see if the asbestos panel is still present. It was put there for a very good reason. Author photo.

On the 100M there is a support running vertically where the air duct meets the cold air box. This support is notched on the 100M. On a standard 100 the strut is straight. Author photo.

The front suspension of these cars uses the lever shock as an upper control arm. The bushings in this arm usually wear and, often, when you think the shock is gone the situation only requires some new bushings. The big story on the early Healeys was the brakes. While the early Triumphs and MG's all had fairly weak brakes in the beginning, no one ever complained about the Austin-Healey brakes. Author photo.

This picture clearly shows the placement of the spare tire, as well as the gas tank, which holds 10½ Imperial gallons of fuel. A constant rumor is that some Austin-Healey 100M's came equipped with racing tires, although no one has ever been able to confirm it. Author photo.

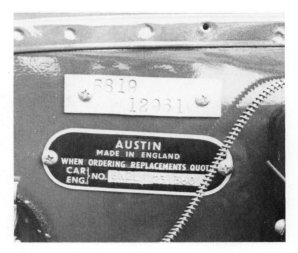

The commission number is on a plate next to the voltage regulator. This plate gives no indication that the car is a 100M. Remember, these cars were simply pulled off the BN2 assembly line and fitted out with the 100M modifications. There was no special serial number sequence. Author photo.

This was the view that most other drivers got of the 100M. Author photo.

CHAPTER 5
100-SIX

SERIAL NUMBERS
Longbridge built - not known - BN4 (2+2 seat)
Abingdon built - 68534-77766 - BN4 (2+2 seat)
         - 501-4650 - BN6 (2 seat)

This is a controversial one. A whole lot of people don't really care for the early 100-Six car at all. The fact that so many people dislike it may very well make it one of the best buys around. The 100-Six was really a step backward for Austin-Healey. When it became apparent that the four-cylinder engine would no longer be available, the decision was made to switch to a six-cylinder. This decision was made by the executives at BMC, not the Healey family. Austin-Healey had become part of the conglomerate and the corporate decisions took away some of the Healey character in this series.

This lack of flavor accounts for one of the reasons that most people just don't like them as much as the earlier cars. Some claim that they feel too heavy and too ponderous. A lot of the heavy feeling depends on what you're used to driving. If you've been driving Buicks, the 100-Six will feel absolutely sporty; whereas if you've been driving Sprites, then be prepared for a big, heavy car.

People who have families larger than two people will find the four-seater a wonderful car. It may also be one of the real bargains of the Austin-Healeys. Being held in low regard by the true Healey fan, it offers a lot of traditional motoring at a lower price.

Just to make matters a little more confusing the BN4 is actually two different cars. The early part of the series was produced at Longbridge and the second batch was produced at Abingdon. The second group is the best of the 100-Six cars. When the production was moved to Abingdon a number of engine modifications were introduced, all improvements.

On the original 100-Six, twin 1½-inch SU H4's were standard equipment, along with the poorest cylinder head ever offered on an Austin-Healey. The whole engine, in fact, was disappointing. Once again only *Autocar* gave the real story. Its testers pointed out that "Although it has, on paper, some 12 bhp in hand over

The grille flash was changed to reflect the new six-cylinder engine. This part is difficult to locate today. A quality restoration should have one attached but if you're simply buying a fun car then you need not worry about items like this. Author photo.

This is the new car. The differences are quite noticeable. First there's the revised hood with the air intake on the front. This change allowed the hood to clear the front of the engine. Geoffrey Healey called it a disguise of necessity. The front grille was revised at the same time. Author photo.

the four-cylinder car, it weighs over three hundred pounds more, and the acceleration figures are not quite so good."

Road & Track had a lot of good things to say about the new engine but went on to print the statistics—statistics don't lie.

	100-Six	100-4	100M	100S
Bhp	102	90	110	132
Curb Wt.	2480	2150	2385	2115
0-40	6.1	6.2	4.7	4.1
0-60	12.2	11.7	9.6	7.8
0-80	22.5	20.8	17.9	13.9
SS 1/4	18.2	18.1	17.4	16.1
Top Speed	105	102	109	119

These figures should only be used as an approximation of what a brand new Austin-Healey could do. There are BN4's around that could blow the doors off a poorly prepared, and driven, 100S. When cars of this type get old, condition is more important than what they could do when new.

The important thing to remember is that when the six-cylinder engine went into the car, the Austin-Healey changed. Maybe the first one, the BN4, wasn't the best example, but it was a new car—a new kind of Austin-Healey.

All of the problems you've heard about the BN4's were recognized by the Healey family. This was especially apparent in competition events. It quickly became obvious that the six-cylinder cylinder head was the major problem, and a newly designed head was developed for racing and rallyes.

This new cylinder head had six port heads and three dual-choke Webers, which made this one of the sexiest-looking Healey engines ever. When the cylinder head was introduced in the road car it reverted back to twin SU's, and was called the Mille Miglia engine.

The confusion begins when this new head, along with the revised camshaft and larger valves, was put into production at the same time as the earlier, less-powerful engine. This new engine was introduced on all the Abingdon BN4's. The other BN4's, built at Longbridge, used the original-style cylinder heads. All the BN6's were built with the improved design.

The solution for identification is to look at the mounting angle of the carburetors. If they're mounted in a vertical position, and the intake manifold is an integral part of the cylinder head you have an early, and poorer engine. If the intake manifold is a removable separate casting and the 1¾-inch SU HD6 carbs mount on a thirty-degree angle, you have the good engine.

The trunk was never too large on an Austin-Healey, especially since all manner of things protruded into the space. All the four-seaters had the spare tire mounted on top of the gas tank, while all the two-seaters had the spare tire mounted behind the seats. Author photo.

The two-tone paint that was first seen on the 100S, and also used on the 100M, was carried over to the 100-Six. Also note that this very early car used drum brakes, as did the entire 100-Six line. Jaguar Cars, Inc., photo.

The exhaust side of the engine displayed dual exhaust manifolds which swept down into twin pipes, continuing the length of the car. *Road & Track* found that, while the exhaust note was pleasant, the most common sound was that of "scraping metal whenever any but the most gradual of driveways is entered." Austin-Healey owners should avoid driving over anything larger than a crushed Marlboro pack.

When *Sports Cars Illustrated* tested the 100-Six in 1959 its drivers found that it could do the quarter mile in 18.8 seconds, and could reach 75 mph. Not content, they returned the following month with a race-prepared Healey and found that it did the standing quarter mile in seventeen seconds flat, and went over 80 mph.

Remember, these were the days when a race car could be driven on the street. You could actually drive a car all week, drive it to the circuit and race the same car. The race car *Sports Cars Illustrated* tested had the competition springs and shocks, all from the Healey catalog, and sixty-spoke wire wheels.

The only changes to the engine were a switch of camshafts and different pistons. And 5500 rpm was used as a red line. The only other difference was a careful balance and assembly. The result was a five-second difference at Lime Rock, where the modified 100-Six could turn 1:15 laps.

Before buying one of these cars be sure you consider that restoration is going to be more difficult than on one of the earlier four-cylinder models. First, everything is going to be bigger. For the average person it is much easier to move a four-cylinder engine around the garage than a six-cylinder version.

There are also more interior parts to purchase than on the BN1's and BN2's. That little seat in the back will cost extra and when you get done, the car will still be worth less than the earlier models. This means the BN4 is hardly a candidate for a total restoration. This is a car to purchase only if it's in reasonably good shape and you intend to enjoy driving it.

The windshield was now fixed in place, as too many customers complained of broken windshields on the previous models. The irony is that the factory actually had to replace more 100-Six windshields than it did on the 100 series. Author photo.

100-Six

ENGINE
TYPE: 6-cylinder
BORE X STROKE: mm/inches: 79.4X88.9/ 3.13X3.50
DISPLACEMENT: cc/cubic inches: 2639/ 160.9
VALVE OPERATION: ohv, pushrod operation
COMPRESSION RATIO: 8.25:1, 8.50:1 for later BN4's and BN6
CARBURETION: twin SU H4, twin SU HD6 for later BN4's and BN6
BHP (mfr): 102 bhp @ 4600 rpm, 117 bhp @ 4750 rpm for later BN4's and BN6

CHASSIS & DRIVETRAIN
TRANSMISSION: 4-speed, overdrive on 3rd and 4th
FRONT SUSPENSION: ind., coil springs, lever arm dampers
REAR SUSPENSION: live axle, half elliptic springs, lever shocks

AXLE RATIO: 4.1:1

GENERAL
OVERALL LENGTH: 13'1.5"
WHEELBASE: 7'8"
TRACK, front: 4'0.75"
         rear: 4'2"
BRAKES, front: drums, 11X2¼"
          rear: drums, 11X2¼"
TIRE SIZE: 5.90X15
WHEEL SIZE: 4.5X15
WEIGHT: 2,435 lbs.

PERFORMANCE (Early Cars)
ACCELERATION: 0-30: 4.3 seconds, 0-60: 12.9 seconds
TOP SPEED: 103 mph

PERFORMANCE (Later Cars)
ACCELERATION: 0-30: 3.6 seconds, 0-60: 11.2 seconds
TOP SPEED: 111 mph

The reflector light was now integrated into the fender panels. The rear lighting arrangement on these cars was probably the simplest and most elegant of all the Austin-Healeys. Author photo.

The front badge was equally simple and used only the signature of the firm plus the famous Healey wings. Author photo.

Very few Austin-Healeys were ever made with disc wheels. While a Triumph or MG looks nice with discs, a Healey looks a little strange. This is a case of rarity not increasing the value of the car. Any Healey with steel disc wheels will sell for less than one with decent wire wheels. Author photo.

If the disc wheels are rare, just imagine how scarce an Austin-Healey hubcap must be. Obviously, make sure that you get all four of them if you buy a disc-wheeled car. Replacing one of these could take some time. Author photo.

SERIAL NUMBERS
101-13750 - 3000 Mark I BN7 (2-seat) and BT7 (2+2 seat)
13751-19853 - 3000 Mark II BN7 (2-seat) and BT7 (2+2 seat)

Introduced in mid-1959, this was the Healey that sealed the reputation—the car many of us think of when we remember macho sports cars from the sixties. In this car, when you made a hard shift into third you could feel the whole chassis twist and shake —the last of the breed. There had been some rough years but now the third act of the Austin-Healey had begun.

A 3000 is quite different from the early 100-4 cars. The amazing thing is that for all of the mechanical differences the character was the same as the first Healeys, and that is what the Austin-Healey is all about: character. When it was introduced no one realized that it would be the final act, all anyone knew was that the car was fantastic.

The interesting thing is that the first 3000 really doesn't look all that much different from the 100-Six that preceded it, but the change in brakes and the improved motor make up for the lack of styling changes. They also make this one of the more desirable Austin-Healeys to own.

A word of caution, though, needs to be added: For all the slings and arrows that have been thrown at the 100-Six, and all the roses that have been bestowed upon the 3000, keep in mind that a lot more depends on the condition of the individual car. It's entirely possible to find a 100-Six that is tighter, faster and handles better than a 3000.

The reverse is also true. When people discuss the merits of the 3000 over the 100-Six they usually talk about two cars that are in very similar condition. It's true that a flawless 100-Six is a better car than a so-so 3000, but seldom will you be comparing the two cars directly. Before you get overly concerned about the type of six-cylinder Healey you're going to buy, think about the condition you want the car to be in. If you are choosing between a 3000 and a 100-Six, of identical condition, take the 3000.

If you intend on holding the car for the next decade maybe there will be a huge gap in appreciation, with the BN7 higher. Most people today, though, buy a Healey to drive, not to decorate the garage.

A car equipped like this one is well worth purchasing. Most owners of the late model cars jump right to the BJ8 series thinking they need all of the luxury. This Mark I has the easy-to-maintain two-carburetor engine and the well-sealed hardtop. It will do everything the BJ8 will do while it retains a sporting flavor lacking in the BJ8. Best of all, a car like this is a lot cheaper than a BJ8. Author photo.

In most shows the early 3000's are even grouped with the 100-Six cars. The dividing line for most Healey fans is at the roll-up windows, where we're talking about a different car. As long as it has a six-cylinder engine up front and Plexiglas windows, it's all the same to most people (purists aside).

When John Christy of *Sports Cars Illustrated* tested one of the first 3000's the most impressive thing he could feel was the extra horsepower (130 bhp versus 117 bhp) and he thought the new 3000 had a lot more torque. These first 3000's had two 1¾-inch SU HD6 carbs on the engine.

The brakes also seemed a lot more powerful on the new car. Healey switched to Girling disc brakes on the front, but kept the same drums on the rear. This change also helped to balance out the braking system a little.

When *Road & Track* got hold of one of the new Healeys they compared times with previous Healey models. Keep in mind that these figures are all for brand new factory cars, not your average 80,000 mile, twenty-five-year-old car.

	3000	100-Six	100-4
0-60	9.8	12.2	11.7
Top Speed	112	105	102

It's interesting to compare these figures with a few other current cars:

	MGA	XK140	TR3A
0-60	14.2	8.4	11.5
Top Speed	105	130	106

When you're shopping for one of the early Austin-Healey 3000's the first thing you should ask is the same as for any other Healey: Are you actually buying what you think you're buying?

The other critical question is, How much of a car am I buying? While all of the parts are currently available, or at least most of them, some are expensive. For instance, that little lower grille lip won't allow you to get much change back from a hundred-dollar bill. The price of all the missing parts can quickly add up.

The other thing to do is to make a thorough rust check. Like all Healeys the 3000's rust just about every place. Lift up the carpets and check the floors, crawl under the car and examine the chassis outriggers and the floor of the trunk.

All of the body panels are available for the car, as are patch panels for the usual rust spots. The fenders also come in fiber glass for the folks who are determined to stop Healey rust permanently. The thing to remember is that these are not easy to get looking right. The same goes for the patch panels.

When it comes to the front suspension the best approach may be to attack it with a whole-suspension rebuild kit. There really isn't a good way to do the front end of this car unless you

The big news for the 1959 Austin-Healey 3000 Mark I was the use of disc brakes on the front wheels. This particular car used the wire wheel option. Also, note that the front suspension is still very similar to the early cars. Author photo.

From the outside there is very little to distinguish the Mark I from the Mark II 3000. The only major difference is the grille. The grille bars on this Mark I 3000 run horizontally, while on the Mark II cars they run vertically. Jaguar Cars, Inc., photo.

do everything, which includes shocks as well. The only problem is that unless you replace the old wire wheels you probably won't notice the difference.

While you're poking around in the engine check the rocker arm shaft. These have a real tendency to wear, throwing all of the valve alignment out of kilter. The rest of the engine is dead reliable, so any of the usual engine checks will be sufficient. Treat it the same as you would any eighty- or ninety-thousand-mile used car.

The rear axle is a real feat to destroy. You almost have to set out with the intent to do it. The most common cause of rear end failure on these early 3000's is that the owner *thinks* something is wrong and attempts to fix it. Unless the gears are properly assembled, there *will* be a real problem. Very few people are very good at rear end work. The best thing to do is to leave it alone. If you're sure there's trouble, then get a professional to do it.

When it comes to side curtains (and this was the last Healey to use them), make sure the frame is in decent shape. Any respectable glass shop can make new sliding panels out of Plexiglas or, better yet, Lexan. If the frames are missing, some parts houses can supply them, or scout the flea markets for a pair with damaged Plexiglas, then repair them yourself.

One of the more desirable options for these early 3000's is the hardtop. If you're looking at a car that has one, you're fortunate. The hardtops for the 3000 and the 100-Six look exactly the same. The only problem is that they don't fit that way. It seems almost impossible to find a hardtop that fits properly, unless it comes attached to the car. With their commonly high prices, be very careful purchasing one at a flea market.

Up to this point I've avoided one of the most important questions, Do you buy a two-seater, or a four-seater (perhaps more correctly, a two-and-one-quarter seater)? A lot of people feel the two-seater is a better buy simply because there are so few of them. Others claim the car just looks better, and since the four-seater's two rear seats are impossible to use, why bother? If I had my choice I would probably take the 2+2 with the hardtop. Second choice would be the two-seater with the drop-top. The choice is really something for warm nights and cold beer; but if a vote were taken, the two-seater would win. When it comes to collecting these cars today, people generally have no strong feeling as to which is better. It probably depends more on their family situation and what is available at the time than different values between the cars.

When you're looking at one of these cars try to find one as fully optioned as possible. The overdrive did not come standard on these cars as it did with the early Healeys, and neither did the wire wheels. The overdrive may not really be necessary, but it

The first series of 3000's had the gearshift off to one side of the transmission tunnel. Author photo.

This picture shows about as clearly as any why Austin-Healeys have never been able to make it up inclined driveways or over any obstacle larger than a pack of cigarettes. This particular exhaust system is connected to a Mark I 3000. Author photo.

will add to the value of the car; but an Austin-Healey with steel disc wheels will never look right.

After a total production run of nearly 14,000 Mark I 3000's, the Mark II was introduced in May of 1961. The Mark II still came in the BN7 (two-seat) and BT7 (four-seat) body styles, but a new grille with vertical slats distinguished the model change. Also, an identification badge above the grille carried a 3000 Mark II designation. But the big news was under the hood. Three, count 'em three, 1½-inch SU HS4 carbs were now mounted on the engine. The only reason that Austin-Healey ever offered this setup was for racing. The FIA ruled that cars could use carb types that were different from the production models, but the *number* of carbs had to be the same.

For racing, the best Austin-Healey setup was the triple Weber arrangement. But this was far too expensive for production. However, if *three SU's* were on the street cars you could use *three Webers* when things got serious.

The problem was that the triple SU's did little for the power on the street car. And when people have one more carburetor to adjust the probability of getting it wrong goes up geometrically. They can be made to run right, but not by an inexperienced person. Since you can't feel the difference in acceleration, why bother? Buy the twin SU Mark I version.

Austin-Healey hardtops were among the finest made. They turned an open sporting car into a high-speed touring car. They're still reasonably priced at flea markets but if you can buy one with your car it's a much better deal. Author photo.

74

Austin-Healey was one of the few manufac-
turers to worry about the structure of its hardtops. This little bar adds a tremendous amount
of support and keeps the top from warping. If
you're missing one, be advised that they're
harder to find than the hardtop itself. Author
photo.

The top support bars are clearly visible from the outside as well.
Most hardtops rely on the Plexiglas rear window to do the job
the struts do in the Austin-Healey top. Author photo.

The correct steering wheel carried a flash on the hub and used wire spokes to connect the hub to the rim. Reproduction steering wheels are now available. Author photo.

The dash, whether a Mark I or Mark II, remained similar to that on previous cars. The steering wheel on this car is not the original wheel but, rather, is typical of what the sporting driver of the sixties felt was required. The overdrive switch is directly behind the steering wheel, between the speedometer and the fuel gauge. Author photo.

Here's an early Mark II 3000 four-passenger model. For the first time there is no identifying mark on the grille. The obvious distinction for the Mark II 3000 is the new-style grille. Another easy way to spot a Mark II 3000 is that the nose badge is colored for the first time. This particular car is a 3000 Mark II from 1961. Jaguar Cars, Inc., photo.

3000 Mark I, BN7 and BT7

ENGINE
TYPE: 6-cylinder
BORE X STROKE: mm/inches: 83.36X88.9/ 3.28X3.50
DISPLACEMENT: cc/cubic inches: 2912/ 177.7
VALVE OPERATION: ohv, pushrod operation
COMPRESSION RATIO: 9.0:1
CARBURETION: twin SU HD, 1¾"
BHP (mfr): 124 bhp @ 4600 rpm

CHASSIS & DRIVETRAIN
TRANSMISSION: 4-speed, optional overdrive on 3rd and 4th
FRONT SUSPENSION: ind., coil springs, lever arm dampers
REAR SUSPENSION: live axle, half elliptic springs, lever shocks

AXLE RATIO: 3.545:1 without overdrive, 3.909:1 with overdrive

GENERAL
OVERALL LENGTH: 13'1.5"
WHEELBASE: 7'8"
TRACK, front: 4'0.75"
rear: 4'2"
BRAKES, front: discs, 11.25"
rear: drums, 11X2¼"
TIRE SIZE: 5.90X15
WHEEL SIZE: 4.5X15
WEIGHT: 2,460 lbs.

PERFORMANCE
ACCELERATION: 0-30: 3.5 seconds, 0-60: 11.4 seconds
TOP SPEED: 114 mph

When the Mark II 3000 was introduced the big change was to three carburetors. The rationale behind this change was that the FIA rules allowed racing cars to be fitted with the same *number* of carburetors as the production cars. Actual street performance didn't change much with the new model. Author photo.

A close-up of the Mark II 3000's vertical grille bars. Also, the nose badge is changed. This front end would continue right through the BJ7 convertible cars. Only with the BJ8 models would this change. Author photo.

The lighting arrangement on the rear of the Healey fenders is always interesting since it changes so often. When the 3000 was introduced the lighting and badge arrangement of the 100-Six was kept and only a 3000 badge was added. Author photo.

The easiest way to identify a Mark II 3000 is by looking inside the cockpit. This is the most elaborate interior to ever appear in an Austin-Healey. Author photo.

The Mark II 3000 even performs the same way the earlier series does. Power was claimed to have risen from 124 bhp at 4600 rpm to 132 bhp at 4750 rpm but this difference wasn't seen in acceleration times. Author photo.

CHAPTER 7
3000 MARK II, MARK III

Mark II ★★★
Mark III ★★★★

SERIAL NUMBERS
BJ7: 17551 to 19853
BJ8 Phase One: 25315 to 26704
BJ8 Phase Two: 26705 to 43026

Now come the elegant Healeys, the refined Healeys—a long way from the early BN1's. The days of fold-down windshields were completely gone. The huge four-cylinder engines and even the drafty side curtains were now also in the past. Healeys have always been as strong as bridge girders. Now they had class as well.

These last Austin-Healeys are really three different cars. The changes were coming quickly at this point: There are the BJ7's (still called a Mark II) and BJ8's (the Mark III), the latter of which came in two forms.

The BJ7 should have been called the Austin-Healey 3000 Mark III, but it wasn't. Donald Healey explained that there were advantages to not calling it a new model; it had something to do with export problems. The new model was simply called the 3000 Sports Convertible and still carried Mark II identification. The British have always called this type of car a drop-head, a name which sounds a little more elegant.

When *Cars* tested this Mark II which was introduced in February of 1962, it found a car capable of over 120 mph. Not only could the car go fast, but it had thick carpets, wind-up windows and a convertible top, not a roadster top, all firmly in place. This was a new era in Austin-Healey history. Not a leap mind you, but the final step in an evolutionary process.

The engine in this car was the BMC three-liter unit of 2912 cc and 136 bhp. The big difference was that the factory went back to installing only two carbs, a decision most people applaud even today. The only reason that the three-carburetor setup was used, as was mentioned in the previous chapter, was for the homologation of three Webers with the FIA racing sanctions. Now the average person could adjust the carbs once again.

Since the new model retained the 3000 Mark II tag officially, most owners seem to have taken to calling them Mark IIA's. Even the nose badge remained the same as on the previous Mark II with side curtains—a rather confusing situation.

The best part of the BJ7 and BJ8 series was that the engine reverted to two carburetors. This made the engine easier to work on, and the power even went up in the BJ8 series. This is the engine from the series that put out 150 bhp at 5250 rpm, while the BJ7 only had 130 bhp at the same rpm. The BJ8 used twin two-inch carburetors while the BJ7 used the 1¾-inch version. Author photo.

Healey had wanted to make even more changes when the BJ7 was introduced but due to declining sales felt it best to rush the new model into existence with just the following changes: wind-up windows, improved steering box, new gearbox case, higher-rate front springs, twin carburetors, convertible top and improved cockpit insulation. Also, the shift lever was moved to the center of the tunnel, and a brake servo became optional.

The other thing was that the two-seater Austin-Healey was now gone. Sales of the model had been dropping for the last several years so when the new model was introduced only the four-seater was available.

The second standard Healey fixture that was, if not missing, in very short supply was the hardtop. In order to install the hardtop the entire convertible top mechanism had to be removed. This effectively discouraged most people from ordering one; and thus, the hardtop is one of the rarest options available for the late model 3000's.

The dash of these cars remained of the traditional pressed steel that was found on the earlier cars. The interesting feature was that for one of the few times in automotive history, this Austin-Healey had a greater speed potential than the numbers on the speedometer would indicate. *Sports Cars Illustrated* clocked 124 mph on a car with a gauge that only read to 120.

The next group of cars incorporated all the features that we've come to identify with the last of the big Healeys. These final changes to the 3000 came in early 1964 with the introduction of the BJ8—the Mark III. They included increased power from twin two-inch SU's, redesigned exhaust system, new dash design, electronic tachometer and vacuum brake servo made standard. The new model also carried 3000 Mark III identification on the hood emblem.

This was it, the final version. Well, almost the final version. The two best parts of the revised car were the dashboard and the exhaust system. Why the factory had waited until 1964 to revise the exhaust system is one of life's small mysteries. Owners of these cars can drive over tiny pebbles without tearing off the whole exhaust system—the only Austin-Healey owners who can be so assured!

The dash is simply elegant. The old steel panel was replaced with wood veneer and a handsome console down the middle of the seats. In some cars the seats were covered in real leather. This is one Austin-Healey in which you can dress for the theater and feel that the car is appropriate.

After only 1,390 Mark III's were produced the factory made even further changes, though only one was terribly significant. These changes were: dropped rear frame, ground clear-

The trunk is the weakest feature of the Austin-Healey. The car is really a GT car but it lacks the room to place anything but a couple of duffle bags. Author photo.

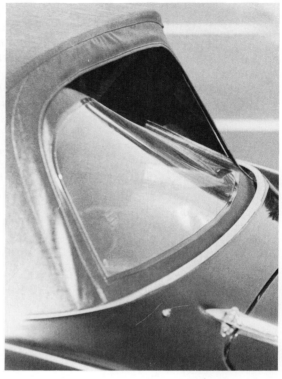

The convertible top and wind-up windows were the big news on the Mark II Sports Convertible with the new BJ7 designation. The windshield was also changed in the process. When the BJ8's were introduced they came with the zipper on the rear window.

3000, Mark II, BN7 and BT7

ENGINE
TYPE: 6-cylinder
BORE X STROKE: mm/inches: 83.36X88.9/ 3.28X3.50
DISPLACEMENT: cc/cubic inches: 2912/ 177.7
VALVE OPERATION: ohv, pushrod operation
COMPRESSION RATIO: 9.0:1
CARBURETION: triple SU HS4 1½"
BHP (mfr): 132 bhp @ 4750

CHASSIS & DRIVETRAIN
TRANSMISSION: 4-speed, optional over-drive on 3rd and 4th
FRONT SUSPENSION: ind., coil springs, lever arm dampers
REAR SUSPENSION: live axle, half elliptic springs, lever shocks

AXLE RATIO: 3.545:1 without overdrive, 3.909:1 with overdrive

GENERAL
OVERALL LENGTH: 13'1.5"
WHEELBASE: 7'8"
TRACK, front: 4'0.75"
    rear: 4'2"
BRAKES, front: discs, 11.25"
    rear: drums, 11X2¼"
TIRE SIZE: 5.90X15
WHEEL SIZE: 4.5X15
WEIGHT: 2,460 lbs.

PERFORMANCE
ACCELERATION: 0-30: 3.7 seconds, 0-60: 11.5 seconds
TOP SPEED: 112 mph

ance increased by one inch, rear spring rate lowered, torque reaction arms on rear axle, strengthened front and rear splined hubs, separate parking and direction indicator lights, larger disc brakes in front and push-button door handles.

These items were all meant for introduction with the start of the Mark III production, but for one reason or another didn't make it. This is the reason for the informal names of Mark III—Phase One and Mark III—Phase Two.

The Phase Two cars are easy to spot, mostly because of the high rear end and the separate turn signals and parking lights. The Phase Two cars have a tremendous amount of clearance between the top of the tire and the rear fender line. The reason for this gap is the revised frame.

When it comes to selecting a car for purchase, the Phase Two cars seem to be the better buy. The reason people love the last Austin-Healeys is that they want the elegant grand tourers. You might as well get the car that has all of the improvements. Why buy the Mark II's and only get half of them?

The interesting thing about these last cars is that they attract a buyer that is totally different from the buyer of the early BN1 cars. The person who buys a BN1 or BN2 is a collector. The person who buys one of these final Healeys is a driver. Neither is really all that interested in purchasing the other type of car.

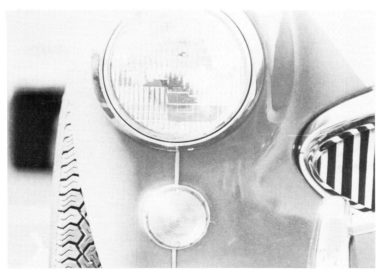

Both the Mark I and Mark II 3000's used a single parking light/turn signal. This particular car is a BJ8 with what appears to be a serious camber problem. Author photo.

If you get really close, the new Mark III badge
will become obvious. Author photo.

The front of the new Mark III was very much the same as it had
been on the last of Mark II 3000's. This would change later with
what became known as the Phase Two cars. The key to identifying
a Mark III is the stunning interior and new top. Jaguar Cars, Inc.,
photo.

The Austin-Healey fan club is made up of several types. A lot of people would never consider having an early car. While most Triumph people would love to have an early TR2, that's not the case with the person who drives a late model 3000. In fact, this owner probably thinks the collectors are rather quaint. A lot of people consider this final batch of cars to be the most desirable Healey ever produced, bar none.

The Mark III—Phase Two cars continued in production until the end and resulted in 17,613 units, ninety percent of which came to the United States. They were the culmination of luxury and performance. A car that began with performance, and little else, had now become a high-speed luxury touring car. And best of all, the character stayed with the car all through the process.

This picture of a Mark III—Phase One car shows how the front of the car was a duplicate of the Mark II 3000. If it weren't for the convertible boot and the roll-up windows you would have to check the instrument panel and nose badge to be sure. Jaguar Cars, Inc., photo.

When the cars came from the factory, the reflectors were installed on the tops of the bumpers. Many owners immediately moved them to below the bumper to give the car a less cluttered look. Today they seem to appear in all sorts of configurations. Author photos.

Two sure ways to tell that you're looking at a Mark III—Phase Two car are the separate turn signal and parking light units, and the gap between the rear fender line and the top of the rear wheel. Author photo.

The real change in the final series of Austin-Healeys came with the dash. The pressed aluminum panel was finally gone. This new wood dash and console ensured that these Healeys would be the most desirable of the big touring Healeys.

3000 Mark III

ENGINE
TYPE: 6-cylinder, in-line
BORE X STROKE: mm/inches: 83.36X88.9/ 3.28X3.50
DISPLACEMENT: cc/cubic inches: 2912/ 177.7
VALVE OPERATION: ohv, pushrod operation valves
COMPRESSION RATIO: 9.0:1
CARBURETION: two SU HS6, 1¾", BJ7; two SU HD8, 2", BJ8
BHP (mfr): 131 bhp @ 5250 rpm, BJ7; 148 bhp @ 5250 rpm, BJ8

CHASSIS & DRIVETRAIN
TRANSMISSION: 4-speed; synchro on top 3
FRONT SUSPENSION: ind. with wishbones, coil springs and sway bar
REAR SUSPENSION: live axle with semi-elliptic leaf springs and sway bar
AXLE RATIO: 3.9:1; 3.55:1 optional

GENERAL
OVERALL LENGTH: 13'1½"
WHEELBASE: 7'8"
TRACK, front: 4'1"
rear: 4'2¾"
BRAKES, front: discs, 11¼"
rear: drums, 11"
TIRE SIZE: Dunlop 5.90X15
WHEEL SIZE: wire wheels standard
WEIGHT: 2,650 lbs.

PERFORMANCE
ACCELERATION: 0-30: 3.6 seconds, 0-60: 9.8 seconds
TOP SPEED: 116 mph

It's hard to believe that this is still the same car from the fifties. What started out as a car with a flexible frame and a big motor ended up as a car with a flexible frame and an even bigger motor. What started out as a sports car ended its life as a high-speed touring car—the Austin-Healey 3000 Mark III—Phase Two. Author photos.

CHAPTER 8
BUGEYE SPRITE

SERIAL NUMBERS
H-AN5-501 to H-AN5-50116

Everyone thought the Bugeye was about the ugliest car they had ever seen. Then BMC came out with the Sprite Mark II and the Bugeye became a legend. This is *the* Sprite to collect. The prices are getting fairly high, considering the humble beginnings of the car, but legends don't come cheap, nor do they ever drop in price.

People always talked about creating a low-priced, fun car; a car that the average person could afford and one that made a person laugh and smile as they drove it down the street. It took BMC and Donald Healey to do it.

The mechanical units for the car came directly from the Austin A35. Up front, Healey used standard A35 coil spring and wishbone components, in conjunction with lever-style Armstrong shocks. The lever arm did double duty as the top arm of the suspension.

The rear suspension is quite interesting since the spring is a quarter-elliptic type, a feature last seen on the Austin Seven. The system puts all the stresses within a very short frame. Each spring has fifteen leaves, and the length from one end to the other is only sixteen inches. It's connected on the chassis end by four studs, with the spring eye formed by two leaves on the axle end. This eye is attached to a bracket that is welded to the axle casing.

The brakes are drum all the way around, the rears being from a Morris Minor. Under the clamshell front end is the real treat from Morris Minor: the 948 cc engine. This was the same engine to later find its way into the Mini and a whole range of specials. For the Sprite, Healey made up a new manifold for two 1⅛-inch SU carbs. In this original form the engine produced 43 bhp at 5000 rpm.

The most surprising thing about the body of the car wasn't its construction as much as the amount of room in the interior. There's a surprising amount of room in these early Sprites. But, like the MGA, it had miserable side curtains and no door handles. The sliding-panel-type side curtains would come a little later for both of these cars. (If I were restoring a Sprite today I would

This was the image: a fun new sports car for fun people. Austin-Healey not only entered a market, it created it. There was no sports car in this class before—there wasn't even a class. It took the old master himself to put a car like this together. From the TR3 taillight to the Austin motor it was all borrowed. Giving people cheap sports cars was the Healey family's specialty. Jaguar Cars, Inc., photo.

certainly cheat on the curtains and go with the later style with the sliding Plexiglas panels.)

The Sprite is quite different from the previous big Healeys, since it has no separate frame. The body and frame are all one. This unit, or monocoque, construction was what made the Sprite possible. It was cheaper to produce a car without a separate chassis. It's also the reason there are so few Sprites around in decent shape. The unit construction traps water, and rust takes hold. When the body panels rust on a Sprite the whole chassis goes limp. This is the major problem on all Sprites; any other problem is far down the list.

Not only will you find rust on most Sprites, you'll also find repairs made by the previous owners, usually multiple layers of plastic putty. The first place to start poking around is the spring boxes. The springs mount in the bulkhead behind the seats. The springs exert a tremendous force on this area and if the boxes are badly rusted then you can count on serious problems.

While in this vicinity also look at the ends of the rocker panels. Now go topside and look at the same areas. Even if you aren't sure what you're looking for, all of this activity will impress the owner and maybe help you to get the price down. If you find a lot of rust in the rocker panel and spring areas make sure that you get the price way down.

The next area is the floor pan. Look to see how much of it has been patched up over the years. New pans are available but they aren't the easiest items to replace since they require welding. Another item that could require some welding is the door pillar area. This area collects moisture, and other general dirt, at the bottom of the door pillars and makes a fine place for rust to begin.

The cars that didn't rust to death were used up by the racers, since the Sprite has been one of the most popular road racing cars around. There are very few straight, rust-free, Bug-eyes left. The ones the rust didn't get, the racers did. This was especially the case with the Sprites with the 948 cc motors. The racers went through these like popcorn.

A lot of people believe that a complete restoration must have this 948 cc motor, so true collectors should look for the 950 that's cast into the side of the block. If you're just buying the car for fun, then the only way to go is with the later-model 1275 cc engine. Install a cam, 1½-inch MGB carbs, and this car will scream.

In the past few years, though, there has been an increasing emphasis on originality with Sprites, so your best bet is to try to find one with as many of the original parts as possible. The most important of these parts is the motor. The 948 cc engines are becoming as hard to locate as the original small carburetors. If

The motor had been used in the Morris Minor from 1952. It was enlarged to 948 cc and found its way into both Morris and Austin sedans, where it was used with a single Zenith carburetor and developed 34 bhp. The Morris Minor used a single SU and got up to 37 bhp. Author photo.

With the addition of twin 1⅛-inch SU's the power went to 43 bhp. What can't be seen in this picture are the heavier valve springs that were added along with the Stellite face exhaust valves and the copper-indium material used for the main bearings. The compression ratio remained the same as it had been in the Morris Minor, 8.3:1. These small carbs are becoming harder to find so if you're intent on having a correctly restored car make sure they come with the car. Author photo.

you can locate a car with these parts intact you will be further ahead in the restoration game.

The best part is that the motor in these little demons is quite easy to work on and the entire unit can be removed with very little strain. You can just put it up on your workbench while you putter away on it. The motor's that small and light.

The original motor is very durable. If it burns oil it's usually the valve guides that are shot. The rings seem to outlast two sets of valve guides. When, not if, you replace them, always use the more expensive, and better, bronze valve guides. You might also want to check the main bearings if the car has more than fifty thousand miles on it. Don't expect them to last forever.

The transmission is easy to rebuild and all the parts are around, although they're getting a little expensive, at least by Sprite standards. For some unknown reason the price of English transmission parts seems to be on a vertical climb. Usually, the synchros are the first to go, followed by bearings. The gears themselves are pretty solid.

The suspension is no real problem unless an owner along the way forgot to use a grease gun on the car. The first thing to go is usually the bushing at the end of the shock arm. This can be rebushed but it's best to simply replace the arm.

Also, check the lower spring platform. These have a tendency to rust and break. It's not a common occurrence, but enough of them have a problem that you ought to check it carefully. Things happen real fast when the front suspension falls off your car!

The best part is that all of the parts are available from the reproduction people. There's very little problem in getting anything from a floor pan to a rear deck lid badge.

An area that's gaining a lot more attention in Sprite collecting is that of factory options. The most noticeable ones are the wire wheels. These do magic things for the appearance of a Bugeye. The car just flat looks better with these hard-to-clean and difficult-to-maintain wheels. What they'll do to extend your weekend cleanup time you can well imagine.

Another option, only available on the later cars, but sold as a dealer-installed option, is disc brakes. What the wire wheels do for the appearance, these do for the stopping power of the Sprite. The only caution should be that they were factory installed on very few cars; only the racers. You should consider this point if in ten years you want to restore the car to the way it left the factory.

One factory option that is even rarer than the disc brakes is the factory hardtop. This was the only hardtop that ever looked right on a Bugeye. The rest all give that homemade appearance.

This is the only Austin-Healey badge not to have the wings attached. It is also currently available on the reproduction market. Author photo.

The Sprite badge for the rear is available on the reproduction market. Almost all of the parts it takes to restore a Sprite are currently available, and at reasonable prices. This makes the Sprite a good car for your first restoration project. Author photo.

The rear of the car was very simple. The taillights are the same as those used on the MGA and the TR3. This makes them easy to find and the price is still cheap. Author photo.

The best way to spot a factory hardtop is to look for the two chrome latches just above the windshield.

The Sprite is one of the few collector cars that can be counted on to appreciate better than the average car. It's also a good car with which to begin your restoration hobby. Everything is so small that it can be easily restored in your own garage, with no hoists or fancy lifting equipment. Just be careful to find one that isn't rusted beyond hope.

Even better than working on one is driving one. They actually encourage all sorts of adolescent behavior. Because the power is so low it's impossible to get in serious trouble. Because they're so small and responsive they do things that no modern computer-designed car can approach.

The motor in the Bugeye feels a lot more powerful than it really is. It has the response that no modern good citizen motor can approach. The only qualification would be that if you like sophistication in a car, avoid the Sprite, any Sprite; they're for fun.

Dealer-Installed Options For The Bugeye

Hardtop	$225	9.3:1 piston set	49
Quick-action filler cap	15	Set of rings for above	8
Lockable filler cap	7	Camshaft (0.315 lift)	32
Wire wheel and disc brake conversion kit	603	Set of inner valve springs & collars	11
8" front drum kit	56	Distributor	37
Antiroll bar	34	Manifold	11
Stiff shock valves (kit)	17	Exhaust pipe	7
Stiff front springs	17	Muffler	8
Stiff rear springs	36	Clips for above	2
Light steel flywheel	142	Dual exhaust system	21
Close-ratio gearbox	290	Thermostat blanking sleeve	1
Parts to convert normal gearbox	66	Large-capacity oil pan	40
5.38 ring and pinion set	27	Oil cooler kit	110
5.38 complete assembly	75	Pair of 1¼" SU carbs	77
4.55 ring and pinion set	20	Manifold for above	30
4.55 complete assembly	75	Polished cylinder head	158
3.73 ring and pinion set	29	Stage V engine, prepared by Donald Healey, ordered as original equipment	$380
3.73 complete assembly	80		

These are the correct wheels and hubcaps for the Sprite. The hubcaps aren't hard to find and the wheels are still around in abundance. Author photo.

Really nice-looking wheels for the Bugeye are the Minilites. They're strong and they look nice. Best of all they're painted magnesium so cleaning them is easy. They're out of production, so when you find a set don't expect them to be cheap. An alternative is the look-alike Panasport wheel. Author photo.

Wire wheels were never factory installed but they were available from the dealer. A lot of them were used by the early racers. They do wonders for the appearance of the car, which is why so many are fitted on Sprites. They also can present all the problems that come with wire wheels, such as broken spokes and out-of-round wheels. Besides, they're so much fun to clean. Author photo.

The interior was about as straightforward and functional as possible. The steering wheel is not original. The original steering wheels are becoming ever more difficult to locate. A grab bar came on the original cars, installed on the lower right of the dash. A lot of these bars were very quickly removed. Author photo.

BUGEYE

ENGINE
TYPE: 4-cylinder, in line, water cooled, cast iron block and cylinder head; BMC Series A
BORE X STROKE: mm/inches: 62.9X76.2/ 2.478X3.0
DISPLACEMENT: cc/cubic inches: 948/57.9
VALVE OPERATION: ohv, pushrod operation
COMPRESSION RATIO: 8.3:1, 9:1 optional
CARBURETION: 2 SU Type H1
BHP (mfr): 43 bhp @ 5200 rpm

CHASSIS & DRIVETRAIN
TRANSMISSION: 4-speed, close ratio optional
FRONT SUSPENSION: ind., coil springs
REAR SUSPENSION: live axle, quarter elliptic springs

AXLE RATIO: 4.22 standard

GENERAL
OVERALL LENGTH: 11'5¼" with front bumper
WHEELBASE: 6'8"
TRACK, front: 3'9¾"
        rear: 3'8¾"
BRAKES, front: drums, 7X1¼"; discs and 8-inch drums optional
        rear: drums, 7X1¼"
TIRE SIZE: 5.20X13
WHEEL SIZE: 3.5X13
WEIGHT: 1,480 lbs.

PERFORMANCE
ACCELERATION: 0-30: 6.0 seconds, 0-60: 23.7 seconds
TOP SPEED: 79 mph

The trick to spotting an authentic Sprite hardtop is seeing the two chrome latches in the front. This is an authentic original owner Sprite with the original side curtains installed. The rubber seal on the bottom of the windshield also appears to be original. Author photo.

In late 1959 or early 1960 a hardtop was offered as an option. It was constructed of fiber glass. Another option offered at the same time was the Plexiglas sliding side curtains. The rear panel slid forward on these screens constructed by Weathershields Ltd. While they were listed as an option most people suspect that every car got them. In March of 1960 they were made standard. Author photo.

This is one of the Sprinzel Sprites that raced at Sebring. A number of these cars were produced by John Sprinzel. Even though the car is often called a Sebring Sprite it raced at several other races, including a number of rallyes. The name came from the number of class victories it scored at Sebring. It could do 0-60 in roughly 10.8 seconds while a normal Sprite would require around 20 seconds to reach the same velocity. Author photo.

One of the reasons that it's so hard to find an original Sprite is that a lot of them ended up being turned into racers. Many former racers have found a new home in Solo II events. One good thing about a former racer is that it was kept out of the snow and salt so it didn't rust. Author photo.

One of the first things most racers did was to change the way the front shell tilted. If done properly, this change makes a lot of sense. Adjusting valves on an original Sprite is like sticking your head into a bear's mouth. You can usually tell original Sprite owners by the bruises on the backs of their heads. Author photo.

CHAPTER 9
SPRITE MARK II

SERIAL NUMBERS
H-AN6-101 to H-AN6-24731
H-AN7-24732 to H-AN7-38828; 1100 engine

They went and changed it. Everybody complained about the stupid headlights and how ugly they looked, so the people at BMC decided to do something about them. They redesigned the Sprite. It even made sense when they did it. What they really did, though, was make those first Sprites classics. The new car was mechanically the same as the first one. What it didn't have was character.

After the Bugeye, the market for Austin-Healey Sprites is totally different. These cars have all of the Bugeye attributes and make a lot of sense as cars for driving around town on a regular basis. They're even good for taking trips. The drawback from a collector's viewpoint is that they don't have those funny headlights.

What they do have is a trunk. This is a real place to put a suitcase and it even has a lid that can not only be opened and closed but locked. Another change was to the front of the car. The wonderful tilting front end was removed, and a conventional front hood took its place. It may have made sense to the people at BMC, but it wasn't as clever. The reality is that the change actually makes working on the engine easier, since you won't have to insert yourself under the clamshell to change plugs and adjust the valves. The conventional hood makes front suspension work a little more difficult, though. On the Bugeye it's all nicely accessible.

The changes other than style were very minor. The close-ratio gearbox became standard. Previously it was only offered as an option for the racing crowd. The other modification was under the new front hood. The carburetors were changed from the 1⅛-inch H 1 SU's to the larger 1¼-inch HS2-version SU's. There were some other alterations made to the engine but all of an internal nature. The combined changes resulted in a total gain of three horsepower.

The big difference came in October 1962 when the motor was enlarged to 1100 cc. A lot of people will tell you that this was a

People complained that the original Sprite looked funny and that it was hard to get your bags out of the car, since it didn't have a trunk lid. So, Austin-Healey changed it. Jaguar Cars, Inc., photo.

SPRITE MARK II 948

ENGINE
TYPE: 4-cylinder, in line, water cooled, cast iron block and cylinder head; BMC Series A
BORE X STROKE: mm/inches: 62.9X76.2/ 2.48X3.0
DISPLACEMENT: cc/cubic inches: 948/57.9
VALVE OPERATION: ohv, pushrod operation
COMPRESSION RATIO: 9:1
CARBURETION: 2 SU Type HS2
BHP (mfr): 49.8 bhp @ 5500 rpm

CHASSIS & DRIVETRAIN
TRANSMISSION: 4-speed
FRONT SUSPENSION: ind., coil springs
REAR SUSPENSION: live axle, quarter elliptic springs
AXLE RATIO: 4.22 standard

GENERAL
OVERALL LENGTH: 11'4"
WHEELBASE: 6'8"
TRACK, front: 3'9¾"
          rear: 3'8¾"
BRAKES, front: drums, 7X1¼"; discs and 8-inch drums optional
          rear: drums, 7X1¼"
TIRE SIZE: 5.20X13
WHEEL SIZE: 3.5X13 steel disc wheels, 4.5X13 wire spokes optional
WEIGHT: 1,500 lbs.

PERFORMANCE
ACCELERATION: 0-30: 5.7 seconds, 0-60: 19.8 seconds
TOP SPEED: 85 mph

change for the worse because of the long stroke in the 1100 cc engine. This poor motor has received more than its fair share of bad reviews.

Actually the only problem the 1100 cc engine really had was that people loved the 948 engines, and the 1275 engine was even better. For several years I raced an 1100 cc engine and had no real problems with the long stroke. If the motor is carefully balanced and carefully put together it's a fine engine. Don't be put off by all the "expert" opinions.

Another change was to the convertible top bows because there was no storage space for them in the new body. The metal bow rods all came apart in the middle now, making the top a little more difficult to put up and take down. The sidescreens that came standard on this car were the same ones that were previously optional on the Bugeye (the thicker, sliding, acrylic type).

In general the Mark II Sprite has all of the mechanical attributes of the Bugeye but lacks the peculiar appearance of the earlier model. It is also a whole lot cheaper than the Bugeye. The problem is that it's going to cost the same amount of money to restore. This means you'll end up putting just as much money into one of these cars but you'll never see the return the way the Bugeye owner will.

These Mark II Sprites are not the best investment, but they'll give you a lot of enjoyment for a minimal amount of money if bought right. The Mark II can be looked on as your basic cheap sports car. When Bugeyes are driven only on sunny weekends you'll still be able to drive your Mark II every day without jeopardizing the family investment.

They also have the most interior room of any of the Austin-Healey Sprites. This is no small matter if you intend to take a trip of over a few hundred miles. As the models progressed, and windows and padded dashes were added, the amount of space dwindled. Not that it's all that bad, it's just that every version of the Sprite seemed to get smaller.

The rest of the Sprites are all in the same category as the Mark II cars. They're for people who enjoy having fun. They've got their money invested in the stock or bond market, and their Sprite is for fun. That's the way it started out, and that's the way it always will be.

The interior in these cars is just as roomy as the Bugeye. It wasn't until the next series that things began to feel really cramped. There's only one really good place to put a radio in these cars and this owner found it. The gearshift knob in this Mark II is not the original nor is the Triumph steering wheel. Author photo.

The car remained very much the same except for the new body style. Here the dash is just as plain as ever and the original steering wheel, with a modern leather cover, looks just as cheap as it did over 20 years ago. Author photo.

SPRITE MARK II 1100

ENGINE
TYPE: 4-cylinder, in line, water cooled, cast iron block and cylinder head; BMC Series A
BORE X STROKE: mm/inches: 64.6X83.7/ 2.54X3.30
DISPLACEMENT: cc/cubic inches: 1098/67
VALVE OPERATION: ohv, pushrod operation
COMPRESSION RATIO: 9:1
CARBURETION: 2 SU Type HS2
BHP (mfr): 56 bhp @ 5500 rpm

CHASSIS & DRIVETRAIN
TRANSMISSION: 4-speed
FRONT SUSPENSION: ind., coil springs
REAR SUSPENSION: live axle, quarter elliptic springs
AXLE RATIO: 4.22 standard

GENERAL
OVERALL LENGTH: 11'4"
WHEELBASE: 6'8"
TRACK, front: 3'9¾"
       rear: 3'8¾"
BRAKES, front: discs, 8¼"
       rear: drums, 7X1¼"
TIRE SIZE: 5.20X13
WHEEL SIZE: 3.5X13 steel disc wheels, 4.0X 13 wire wheels optional
WEIGHT: 1,560 lbs.

PERFORMANCE
ACCELERATION: 0-30: 5.4 seconds, 0-60: 18.3 seconds
TOP SPEED: 85 mph

SPRINZEL SPRITE PERFORMANCE
ACCELERATION: 0-40: 5.8 seconds, 0-60: 10.8 seconds
TOP SPEED: 100 mph

The 948 cc Mark II's used the same rear suspension as the Bugeyes. The area where the spring mounts to the chassis is prone to rust and should be looked at before any money changes hands. Rust here could get serious. Author photo.

The Mark II Sprite will never be a serious collector car, so turning it into a Solo I car is not a major crime. It's a lot of fun and not very expensive to maintain. Author photo.

The front wheel opening never received the lip that the rear one had. Also, the lower seam, just behind the tire, served no purpose other than as a great place for rust to form. When the Sprite starts to rust it will begin in the lower panel and in the pillar directly below the windshield. One reason for the pillar to rust is that the rubber seal under the windshield post develops leaks, letting water run down into the chassis. This rubber mounting pad should be replaced if the original pad is still in place. Author photo.

The Mark II Sprite picked up the family theme with the MGB-style taillights. Also notice the stiffening lip that was added to the rear wheel opening. It would never again match the front wheel opening. In addition, the sliding Plexiglas sidescreens that were an option on the Bugeye became standard from the factory. Author photo.

SERIAL NUMBERS
H-AN8-38829 to H-AN8-64755

The Spitfire was closing in and it was time to make some more changes. It was time to install windows that could be rolled up and down, which meant that the windshield should be changed— and why not the dash as well? BMC was playing catch up and the Sprite was becoming civilized.

The Sprite Mark III is one of those strange cars that is neither here nor there. The car was starting to lose some of the frivolity of the early models, yet it was resisting real improvements. The ride was still rough and the engine and transmission just as noisy as ever.

The biggest mechanical change was in the design of the rear springing. The previous Sprites all had quarter elliptic springs. The front of the spring was attached to the chassis and the spring stopped at the axle attachment point. On the Mark III it continued to a point on the rear of the chassis, one-half elliptic spring.

The only real difference this makes in driving the car is that the later Sprites do not feel as twitchy as the earlier ones. For most people any Sprite will feel twitchy; it's likely been a long time since they have driven a small car that was designed for performance.

The performance and the noise are two things that most people notice the first time they drive a Sprite. The cars have never been quiet, and for some reason the Mark III's seem to be even noisier. A lot of people think the transmission is going bad just because it makes so much noise. A friend once sold me a Sprite because he figured the gearbox was bad. Now, 10,000 miles later, the gearbox still hasn't been out of the car.

The Mark III Sprite has to be viewed not as a logical development of the car but rather as an answer to the Triumph Spitfire. By this time the Spitfire was winning on the showroom floor. People liked things such as windows that rolled up and down.

This Sprite was a real rush job by BMC engineers since they didn't even bother to redesign the top into a true converti-

The Sprite was becoming refined. It still looked the same from the front; but only from that angle. If you look carefully you'll see that the windshield is different from the one on the Mark II. Author photo.

ble. While the windows worked just like in a modern car, the top was strictly erector-set technology. Actually, though, this is not all bad. Who even bothers with the top on a Sprite today? And the car actually looks better without the folded top that finally arrived on the Mark IV. All of the criticisms about the windows and top don't apply as much today as they did fifteen years ago.

Remember, the people who bought this car new didn't buy it as a fun car to have for nice days. They usually bought it as an only car. This was what was going to get them to work and to the grocery store; and the same one that they would take on vacation. The Sprite was an all-purpose everyday car. *Road & Track* said it offered more fun per dollar than any car it could name, provided the car was accepted for what it was.

This is also how you should look at the car today. There is very little traditional collector value in this car. On the other hand there is a lot of fun left in it. Side curtains may be traditional and they may be very British, but they are not very pleasant to live with on a daily basis. Think of the windows as a luxury, and the top as a reminder of traditional British engineering.

The new vent windows give the whole thing away. Author photo.

Previous Bugeye and Mark II Sprites used a quarter-elliptic leaf spring (shown to the left). The new half-elliptic design resulted in better axle location and slightly improved handling, neither of which is noticeable on the average well-worn, oft-abused old Sprite.

SPRITE MARK III

ENGINE
TYPE: 4-cylinder, in line, water cooled, cast iron block and cylinder head; BMC Series A
BORE X STROKE: mm/inches: 64.6X83.7/ 2.54X3.30
DISPLACEMENT: cc/cubic inches: 1098/67
VALVE OPERATION: ohv, pushrod operation
COMPRESSION RATIO: 9:1
CARBURETION: 2 SU Type HS2
BHP (mfr): 59 bhp @ 5750 rpm

CHASSIS & DRIVETRAIN
TRANSMISSION: 4-speed
FRONT SUSPENSION: ind., coil springs
REAR SUSPENSION: live axle, half-elliptic springs

AXLE RATIO: 4.22 standard

GENERAL
OVERALL LENGTH: 11'4"
WHEELBASE: 6'8"
TRACK, front: 3'9¾"
        rear: 3'8¾"
BRAKES, front: discs, 8¼"
        rear: drums, 7X1¼"
TIRE SIZE: 5.20X13
WHEEL SIZE: 3.5X13 steel disc wheels, 4.0X 13 wire wheels optional
WEIGHT: 1,560 lbs.

PERFORMANCE
ACCELERATION: 0-30: 5.4 seconds, 0-60: 18.3 seconds
TOP SPEED: 85 mph

Windows that roll up and down—that's what the Mark III Sprite is all about. The handy door bins were lost in the process but most people never missed them. The upholstery panels are all currently available. Author photo.

Austin-Healey also upgraded the dash panel. Competition in the market for small sports cars was becoming stiff between Triumph and the Spridgets, as they had now become known. Every time one company would upgrade its product the other would follow in rapid succession. Author photo.

The Mark III used the wrongly maligned 1100 cc engine. These engines hold up very well under normal use and few owners have had all the problems that are much discussed. This is also the first engine to use the PVC valve. Author photo.

The Sprite badge on the rear deck lid is also available from a variety of parts suppliers. Author photo.

The badge on the front hood remained the same as it had been on the Mark II. These are available on the reproduction market. Author photo.

The rubber grommet around the gas tank filler neck is another item that is usually rotted, and in generally sad shape. Once again it's cheap and easy to replace. The taillights, though, are starting to get rather expensive, especially the chrome piece. Author photo.

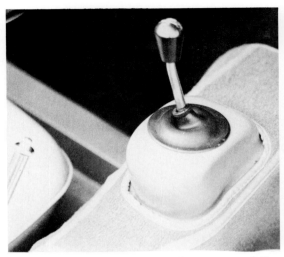 

The transmission remained the same and the gearshift lever did likewise. On a lot of these cars the rubber boots are torn and cracked. These should be replaced since they let fumes into the car. Considering how inexpensive they are there's no reason to end up smelling like oil every time you go for a ride with the top up. Author photo.

These leather straps were used on all the Sprites as door stops. Most of them have rotted away and now every time someone opens the door it bangs into the side panel. This should be one of the first items to replace in any Sprite. Author photo.

The rubber plugs are used to cover a jacking point. These usually rotted away a decade ago. Clean the inside of this area thoroughly and buy some new rubber plugs. Author photo.

The chrome piece for the parking light/turn signal looks just like the one on the Austin America; it isn't. But it is one of those items that seems expensive considering that it's a Sprite part. Author photo.

The panel right behind the wheel and below the fender line rusts very quickly. It should be cleaned and painted from the rear on a regular basis. Author photo.

The heater duct should be checked carefully for leaks. If it's full of holes or, worse yet, missing, then every time you use the heater you'll just be filling the car with fumes from under the hood. Author photo.

SERIAL NUMBERS
H-AN9-64756 to H-AN9-85286

These were the best of the Sprites. These were the worst of the Sprites. Just after we got the best motor ever put in an Austin-Healey Sprite we got the emission control laws in the United States. It was a case of going from the good to the bad and, finally, the ugly. The only good part was BMC killed the Sprite before it had a chance to look like the final MG Midget, sitting up on stilts and carrying funny rubber bumpers on either end.

The motor for the Mark IV came from the Mini Cooper S. It lost a few horsepower in the translation but it was still the finest motor to ever find its way into a Sprite. As the car moved into its later years the American emissions laws came into effect. The 65 bhp of the early units allowed the Sprite to effectively compete with the Spitfire, and without straining anything. The 1967 Sprite was the fastest Sprite ever produced.

The original plan had been to use the full-blown Mini motor with 76 bhp, but the result would have blown the MGB away. That simply was not to be allowed. The fun part is that with very little work the Mark IV Sprite can be modified even today so that it will leave stock MGB's in the dust. There's a ton of parts available for these cars, most of them fairly reasonably priced.

You really don't need the Weber carburetion setup, though. This applies to all the Sprite engines. The way the cylinder head is designed, a Weber won't produce any more power than a larger pair of SU's. It's fairly easy to mount MGB carbs on a Sprite engine and the power will be as good as, if not slightly better than, with a single Weber. Plus, it's a whole lot cheaper.

There's a consensus that the Mark IV cylinder head is the best A Series cylinder head ever developed. Even though many people were upset that the Cooper S head wasn't installed on the Mark IV cars, the Sprite head has turned out to be more reliable. The cylinder head on the Cooper S develops cracks between the two valves. For all the complaining when the car was introduced these Mark IV, pre-emission heads are now installed on a lot of racing Minis. There has to be some irony in that.

The Mark IV is actually easier to spot with its top down. The top folds back in a bundle just like any other convertible top. The only problem is that it cuts into the luggage space behind the seats. When buying a Mark IV, try to find one with a boot or tonneau cover in decent shape since they're not cheap anymore. The rest of the car has all of the problems with rust that the earlier cars had. Jaguar Cars, Inc., photo.

This is the real reason for buying a Mark IV. The 1275 cc engine is the strongest engine found in any Sprite. In the United States try to find a 1967 model. The ones that followed had all sorts of emissions equipment attached, and the cars suffered. Driving a 1967 model Sprite is probably more fun than you've had in a long time. After too many years of driving slow, stodgy cars you'll find that the Sprite feels like a rocket. Jaguar Cars, Inc., photo.

The other good thing, at least in retrospect, was the decision to lower the compression on the Sprite. Given the quality of today's gasoline it now makes sense. The only bad point was that BMC also lowered the quality of some components such as the crankshaft. In the Mini a nitrided steel crank was used, but the Sprite got a forged one.

The new convertible top on the Mark IV was a huge success and is really quite convenient, but most of them have been ruined in the folding process. It seems you have two choices with this top: First, you can install it, keep it erected, and have a flawless top. Second, you can lower it but be assured that it will eventually get neat little tears in it and the plastic windows will be scratched. The area behind the cockpit was made slightly larger to hold this top equipment and a nice boot was installed to cover it; if you're able to pull and stretch hard enough to get it to fit. Generally, leaving it out in the sun to make it flexible will do the job.

The car to have in this series is the 1967 model. This was the last year before the air pump became standard equipment. This was, as mentioned earlier, the fastest Sprite ever produced. The Sprite was never considered a fast car in its time but driving one of the 1967's today sure is a whole lot of fun.

Just after the Mark IV was introduced the development work for the series was turned over to the folks at MG. The work of the Healeys was over. There was no place for them in the huge conglomerate. In 1968, Standard-Triumph would be brought into the fold and the Spitfire and Spridgets would be produced by the same company and compete for the same buyers. The efforts of the Healey family had been magnificent, the best part was that they left when the cars were still fun. What happened after they left is best explained by the MG fans. Donald Healey was never to become a part of the joke that the final Midgets became.

SPRITE MARK IV

ENGINE
TYPE: 4-cylinder, in line, water cooled, cast iron block and cylinder head; BMC Series A
BORE X STROKE: mm/inches: 70.61X81.28/ 2.78X3.20
DISPLACEMENT: cc/cubic inches: 1275/77.8
VALVE OPERATION: ohv, pushrod operation
COMPRESSION RATIO: 8.8:1; 8.0:1 optional
CARBURETION: 2 SU Type HS2
BHP (mfr): 65 bhp @ 6000 rpm

CHASSIS & DRIVETRAIN
TRANSMISSION: 4-speed
FRONT SUSPENSION: ind., coil springs
REAR SUSPENSION: live axle, half-elliptic springs
AXLE RATIO: 4.22 standard on early cars, 3.9:1 from 77573

GENERAL
OVERALL LENGTH: 11'5½"
WHEELBASE: 6'8"
TRACK, front: 3'9¼"
    rear: 3'8¾"
BRAKES, front: discs, 8¼"
    rear: drums, 7X1¼"
TIRE SIZE: 5.20X13 standard, 145X13 radial ply optional
WHEEL SIZE: 3.5X13 steel disc wheels, 4.5X13 wire spoked optional
WEIGHT: 1,560 lbs.

PERFORMANCE
ACCELERATION: 0-30: 4.2 seconds, 0-60: 14.7 seconds
TOP SPEED: 100 mph

The interior panels stayed the same but the seats were upgraded. The additional padding actually makes the interior seem more crowded than the earlier models. Getting into one with the top up is for agile people only. Author photo.

The new dash panel also seems to make it feel a little more crowded. The radio console is a nice touch. There's really no sense at all in having a quality radio in one of these cars, though, since you won't be able to hear it over the exhaust, wind and transmission noise. Author photo.

CHAPTER 12
JENSEN-HEALEY

The Jensen-Healey was really the consolidation of the old alliance with the Jensen factory. This was a modern Healey. The demise of the big Austin-Healey in 1968 was a sad day. People had always held the car in high regard, and still feel that it was the finest example of the postwar British sports car era.

The inability of British Leyland to even come close to a new Healey was long felt in the United States. Austin-Healey fans just never regarded the Triumph TR6 as a suitable alternative. They felt the car never really had the necessary power.

One such individual was Kjell Qvale, at the time president of British Motor Car Distributors, Inc., in San Francisco. He had managed to make a small fortune importing British cars into the United States and had a very good idea of what the American public wanted.

Armed with this knowledge, he went to see his old friend, Donald Healey, with the proposal that they design and build a new open sports car that could be developed and sold on an independent basis (that is, free of the problems that British Leyland was having).

The result of this idea was the Jensen-Healey. Donald Healey and his son, Geoffrey, put together a styling model along with some suggestions regarding the mechanical components that would be used. At the same time, Jensen Motors was contacted to do the detail design and to set up a manufacturing operation. This was a natural relationship since Jensen was the company that built the bodies for the big Healeys, as well as the Volvo P1800 and the Sunbeam Tiger.

This choice became even more sensible when Kjell Qvale bought a majority interest in the Jensen works and became president of the firm. Donald Healey was made chairman of the board and Geoffrey a board member. To round out the company Albert Vickers, formerly of Rolls-Royce, was also placed on the board.

The idea was that this would be a very straightforward car with an engine in the front and the rear wheels driving. The steering and front and rear suspension would be taken from the Vauxhall Firenza. The engine would come from Lotus, which had a new 140 bhp, sixteen-valve, dohc slant four, which Healey

The interior of these cars is really quite comfortable—actually nicer than the old 3000's. The only major problem in the cars is that the wood strip on the dash begins to peel away and look messy. Author photo.

connected to a Chrysler gearbox, taken from the Rapier H120.

The body was of unitary design built by welding together a number of small pieces. Using this design, the company could avoid the cost of large presses necessary for the large body panels. The smaller pressings could be done by any number of small British firms.

The best part of the two-liter Lotus motor was that it was designed around the American emission requirements, and Lotus felt it could easily produce the required 20,000 units each year. The motor was angled at forty-five degrees to the left side, leaving a fair amount of room under the hood. The English Jensen-Healeys got a pair of Dellorto carbs, very similar to Webers, and the American market got a pair of Strombergs.

There was said to be very little difference, none on paper, between the two engines. Since very few people have ever driven the two versions side by side, and no one has measured the horsepower on the same dyno, you'll just have to accept the factory's word. When *Road & Track* tested the car in late 1972 the engine performance was compared to the Triumph TR6, the Alfa Romeo 2000 GTV and the Datsun 240Z. It came close, but not equal, to the Lotus Elan. This was the European specification car.

When *Road & Track* drivers finally got a federal specification car to test, they found the power to be down, but felt that it still compared favorably to other two-liter cars. The worst part of the motor was that it made so much noise. They felt that it sounded a lot like an MGB, hardly the sort of comment that the folks at Jensen-Healey were looking for.

When it came to the ride, *Road & Track* felt there was a big difference between the MGB and the Jensen-Healey. The Jensen-Healey was found to have the cornering power of a Pantera, and even close to the Lotus. At the same time the ride was most comfortable. The only problem *Road & Track* found with the car was that it was so routine: "To remember the originality, the impact, the appeal of the original Austin-Healey is to know and regret that the Jensen-Healey is only competitive with the cars in its class."

The real problem would come later. The car had far more troubles than the others in its class. In 1973, *Autocar* described the Jensen-Healey as "Engine by Lotus; Gearbox by Vauxhall; Development by customers?" After driving the car for some 10,000 miles its testers found themselves rather disappointed. With just 800 miles on the clock the car started to blow smoke. By the time they got to 1,100 miles they were adding oil at the rate of a quart every 300 miles. Finally at 1,600 miles Jensen replaced the engine.

The Jensen-Healey never had really small bumpers but they grew as the car continued in production. This is a 1975 version. Most of the quality control problems were being brought under control by this time and this particular car had no rust. All the early cars were convertibles. A hardtop was made optional, but very few of them are around. Author photo.

The taillight design also remained constant through the history of the Jensen-Healey. This is the 1975 rear bumper with the Jensen-Healey name embossed in the rubber. Author photo.

A few hundred miles after this the universal joint on the forward end of the driveshaft gave out. All of this might have been excusable but the car started to visibly rust after only a few months. Sure, all cars rust, but most don't do it in the first year of ownership. Then the top started leaking water, which led *Autocar* to conclude that the top was inferior to that on the previous Austin-Healeys.

Just about this time, the car went back into the shop for its third engine in less than a year due, again, to oil consumption. At the close of the article they added the final blow in relating that their experiences with the car were by no means unique. In fact, when *Motor* did a survey of owners, it had to add a new category for the number of days the car spent in the shop. Thirteen percent of the owners had their cars in for longer than a month.

It was inevitable that people would compare this new Jensen-Healey to the fondly remembered Austin-Healey. Both *Cars and Car Conversions* and *Wheels* ran such a test. The first difference was noticed by *Cars and Car Conversions* when they tried to drop the top on the Jensen-Healey. It took four times as long as it did on the older Austin-Healey 3000. This area, though, was just about the only one in which the older car excelled. They found that once the character and good looks of the 3000 were laid aside the Jensen-Healey was a far better car. They just wished that it hadn't looked like a blown-up Spitfire.

What does all of this mean for today's buyer? Probably not a whole lot, since many of the early problems were taken care of by the factory. The best place to begin your inspection of a Jensen-Healey is at the back of the car where the rust usually starts. Look for rust along the top of the fenders and in the trunk area. If you find rust here, it is usually an indication of deeper trouble underneath. Rust will also form along the tops of the front fenders, near the hood opening. In more severe cases it will also be found along the bottoms of the fenders and in the rocker panels.

When it comes to the underside, check the rear axle radius arm mountings. While you're looking for rust, also check the bolts, since they seem to loosen and tear up the bushings. In the front, check the steering column—the lower nylon bushes tend to deteriorate, the result of the two-piece steering column being too close to the exhaust system. One bright spot is that the front suspension should be relatively free of problems.

The engine is not quite so trouble free. Most of the difficulties are in the top end of the engine. Always be careful when you tighten the cam covers; a zealous mechanic can actually bend the metal covers.

Motor magazine found the ride and handling of the 1975 model to be impressive; and praised the improved finish. The gearbox in these cars is a five-speed from Gertag, the same transmission as is found in some of the BMW's. Author photo.

The other thing you should do as soon as possible is to replace the rubber-toothed timing belt. This has a given life span and, unlike a timing chain, doesn't make any noise before it goes bad—just one quick break and it's all over. When the belt breaks it usually means a lot of the valves will go with it, so it's best to replace it on a regular basis.

There are a number of Jensen-Healeys floating around on the used car market but the enthusiasm for them is not very great. Outside of the noisy motor they're not all that bad of a car. The most common complaint heard about the Jensen-Healey is that it lacks character. Character doesn't get you back and forth to work every day, and neither does it make working on the car any easier. Just think of the Jensen-Healey as a pleasant modern sports car and you won't be disappointed. If you buy a Jensen-Healey as a collector car, though, you'll be making a serious mistake. It will never begin to approach the value of an Austin-Healey.

JENSEN-HEALEY

ENGINE
TYPE: dohc inline 4-cylinder, water cooled
BORE X STROKE: mm/inches: 95.2X69.3/ 3.75X2.73
DISPLACEMENT: cc/cubic inches: 1973/121
VALVE OPERATION: dual overhead camshafts
COMPRESSION RATIO: 8.4:1
CARBURETION: twin Dellortos, English; twin Stromberg-Zenith, American
BHP (mfr): 140 @ 6500 rpm

CHASSIS & DRIVETRAIN
TRANSMISSION: 4-speed
FRONT SUSPENSION: upper A-arms, lower lateral arm, compliance struts, coil springs, tube shocks
REAR SUSPENSION: live axle on trailing arms, upper control arms, coil springs, tube shocks

AXLE RATIO: 3.73:1

GENERAL
OVERALL LENGTH: 92"
TRACK, front: 53.5"
       rear: 52.5"
BRAKES, front: discs, 10.0"
        rear: drums, 9.0X1.75"
TIRE SIZE: 185/70 HR13 Pirelli
WHEEL SIZE: 5.5X13 aluminum alloy
WEIGHT: 2,155 lbs.

PERFORMANCE
ACCELERATION: 0-30: 2.8 seconds (English), 3.7 seconds (American); 0-60: 8.1 seconds (English), 9.7 seconds (American)
TOP SPEED: 125 mph (English), 115 mph (American)

The original cars with the smaller bumpers used a different front turn signal arrangement. Author photo.

The body panels remained the same throughout the production of the car. This makes the parts situation better than might be expected. The parking light/turn signal units were changed when the larger bumpers were added. Author photo.

These wheels were standard on the Jensen-Healey. A few prototypes used the Lotus wheels, but they were never a production item. Author photo.

Every magazine that tested one praised the car. The only problem was, and still is, the motor. The engine was just too noisy for a serious GT car. If you find one on the market today you can have a rare car with almost none of the usual parts problems, since almost all of the parts interchange with the convertible models. The car will at least hold its own in price but don't look for tremendous appreciation. The Jensen-Healey GT is virtually unknown outside of the Jensen-Healey circle of friends. Jensen Motors, Inc., photo.

The American version got the Strombergs, while the rest of the world got the Dellorto carburetors. The factory claimed the horsepower was the same but no magazine in the United States was able to match the times of the cars tested by the English drivers. It really isn't worth the bother of fitting a set of Dellortos or Webers to a Jensen-Healey—the expense will be too great to justify. If you need parts for the engine a Lotus dealer is a very good source, since the engine is used in the Lotus line as well. Author photo.

SERIAL NUMBERS & MODEL DESIGNATIONS

The confirmed Austin-Healey fan will tell you that there is nothing complicated about the way the various Austin-Healey models were designated and given serial numbers. All that means is that they have spent some time learning the system. Most people find it confusing. In fact, a lot of people who own Healeys find it all very confusing.

The first step is to remember that all the big Healeys begin with the letter B. This was merely Austin's way of recording that the engine was between two and three liters in displacement.

Next, N, T or J will always be the second letter in the model designation. The N refers to a two-seater and the T refers to a four-seater. When the letter J was used it meant the car was a convertible.

This method seems all very logical until you realize that the BN4 is a four-seater car. The only answer is that no one really believed it was a four-passenger car when it was brought out—another basic Austin-Healey mystery.

Following the three letters will be a number. This simply means which car in the series it is. The BN2 was the second of the series. The BJ8 was the eighth of the series. This all gets confusing when you realize that the BJ7 should have really been an 8, but for reasons connected with the racing program, it remained a 7. No one ever said the Austin-Healey history was logical, just easy to understand.

When it comes to the Sprites the process is equally easy to understand. The first letter, H, indicates that the car is a Healey. The second letter in the series tells you that the car uses an A Series engine. The third letter, which will always be an N, means that the car is a two-seater, just the same as the N in the large Healey series.

The fifth character will always be a number and indicates the series of the car. The Bugeye was the fifth of a series, at least from the Austin viewpoint. The final series of Sprites was a 10. Hence, the serial number H-AN 10. This was also the designation for the Austin Sprite, even if the Healeys were gone from the company at that time, and the Healey name had been removed from the nameplate.

The Austin-Healey Sprite Mark V never made it into the United States and only the Midget was sold to the Americans. The same was true of the Austin Sprite. The last Sprite was built in July 1971, but for the Americans that date was really the introduction of the 1969 models.

When it comes to the racing cars and the 100S cars, the system gets a little more confusing. Donald Healey actually set out to confuse people with the serial numbering system for the 100S. The numbers skipped about to make it difficult to ascertain how many had actually been manufactured. Fooling the FIA has been a long and honorable practice among racers.

Anyone buying a former factory race or rally car is strictly on his own. These cars went through a variety of motors and, in some cases, bodies. Graham Robson lists the registration numbers in his book, but even this system is questionable. The best advice is to see if the car has a continuous history. If there are gaps in the history then you should begin to wonder if you're looking at an authentic car. You will pay extra money for one of these cars so make sure you pay extra attention to what you're buying.

PRODUCTION RECORDS

BIG HEALEYS

100	BN1	10,688	1953 to 1955
100	AHS	55	1955
100	BN2	3,924	1955 to 1956
100-Six	BN4	10,286	1956 to 1959
100-Six	BN6	4,150	1958 to 1959
3000 Mk I	BN7	2,825	1959 to 1961
3000 Mk II	BN7	355	1959 to 1961
3000 Mk I	BT7	10,825	1959 to 1961
3000 Mk II	BT7	5,095	1961 to 1962
3000 Mk II	BJ7	6,113	1962 to 1963
3000 Mk III—Ph I	BJ8	1,390	1963 to 1964
3000 Mk III—Ph II	BJ8	16,314	1964 to 1968
3000 Rally cars	BJ8	7	

SPRITES

H-AN5	8,729	1958
	21,566	1959
	18,665	1960
	39	1961
H-AN6	10,020	1961
	10,430	1962
H-AN7	1,611	1962
	8,852	1963
	752	1964
H-AN8	10,405	1964
	8,882	1965
	6,616	1966
H-AN9	406	1966
	6,895	1967
	7,049	1968
H-AN10	6,129	1969
	1,292	1970

RECOMMENDED READING

BOOKS

Austin-Healey "Frogeye" Sprite
By Lindsay Porter

This was the first book devoted only to the earliest series of Sprites. It's an excellent book to have on your shelf regardless of which Sprite you own. Since the motors and chassis remained virtually the same for the entire run of the car the hints from one model apply to the others as well.

Austin Healey Sprite 1958-1971
Austin Healy 100 & 3000 Collection No. 1
Austin Healey 100 1952-1959
Austin Healey 3000 1959-1967
Jensen-Healey 1972-1976
Brooklands Series edited by R. M. Clarke

This is an excellent series of books that puts all the old articles in one handy place. The series reprints articles from most of the major automotive magazines in the English-speaking world. These include not only the road tests, but some of the historical articles as well. The only problem is that they miss some very good articles by not using the old *Sports Car Graphic* and *Motor Trend*.

Healey: The Handsome Brute
By Chris Harvey

The quality of the production is flawless. The pictures are lovely and the whole book is simply marvelous. The only problem is that a lot of people feel too many factual errors crept into the text. It's still a lovely place to begin your Austin-Healey education.

Austin Healey: The Story of the Big Healeys
By Geoffrey Healey

This is one book that every Healey owner ought to have on his or her bookshelf. It won't help you to keep the car running, but it will help you understand the history of the car sitting in your garage. The best part of the book is the inside perspective about why your car was designed and constructed the way it was.

The Big Healeys: A Collector's Guide
By Graham Robson

This is another one of the books that every Healey owner, or potential owner, ought to keep around the house. The book has a very distinctive English approach. Fans in the United States might wish for a little better coverage on the American scene, but it's still a book you should own.

The Sprites and Midgets: A Collector's Guide
By Eric Dymock

This is the only book currently available that covers all of the Spridgets. It follows the same format as all of the other Collector's Guides but has the added bonus of being one of the best written in the whole series. If you're considering the purchase of a Spridget then get this book first.

Tuning BL's A-Series Engine
By David Vizard

If David Vizard says it works on an Austin-Healey Sprite engine, believe it. Vizard probably knows more about the Sprite engine than any other person in the world. If you're rebuilding your Sprite engine, consider this book as valuable as the factory manual. If you want more horsepower, consider it even more valuable.

Road & Track on Austin-Healey 1953-1970

Collections seem to be very popular. This is *Road & Track's* answer to the Brooklands series. The problem is that it only contains *Road & Track* articles. The good part is that the reproduction is far superior to the Brooklands series; it doesn't make you think you're reading a Xerox of the original.

MG Midget & Austin-Healey Sprite: Guide to Purchase and D.I.Y. Restoration
By Lindsay Porter

What Vizard does for the Sprite engine, Porter does for the entire car. The big problem is that most of the book deals with body-work. It will never replace a friend who's already been through the process of rebuilding a Sprite. If you plan on working on a Sprite this book is useful, just don't plan on it solving all your problems.

Austin-Healey 100: The Original 4-Cylinder Models
By John Wheatley
Here's one of the Super Profile series that does a nice job with the early Healeys. This is a basic primer on the early cars and has some very nice color pictures.

MG Midget/Austin Healey Sprite
By Lindsay Porter
Here we find all the non-Bugeye Sprites. The book is exactly like the others in the Super Profile series. It has some nice color photos and a very basic description of the later Sprites.

PERIODICALS
Autoweek
965 E. Jefferson
Detroit, MI 48207
(313) 567-9520
published weekly
This tabloid-sized newspaper deals with a variety of automotive hobbies. The classified ads carry a full range of Austin-Healeys and have the best selection of racing Austin-Healeys of any publication. This is just the thing if you're looking for a Solo II or road racing Austin-Healey.

Car and Driver
2002 Hogback Road
Ann Arbor, MI 48104
(313) 944-0055
published monthly
This was formerly called *Sports Cars Illustrated* and covered every Austin-Healey ever produced. Coverage of Austin-Healeys stopped when production ceased and seldom do any historical articles appear.

Automobile
120 E. Liberty Street
Ann Arbor, MI 48104
(313) 994-3500
published monthly
David E. Davis was the former editor of *Car and Driver*. The focus is upscale, modern cars. The magazine is modeled after *Car* magazine in England. Don't expect to find too much about Austin-Healeys in this magazine.

Classic and Sportscar
Haymarket Publishing Ltd.
12-14 Ansdell Street
London W8, England
This is one of the better English magazines. While it does very little on the Austin-Healeys, it's still a very good publication for keeping up with the English car scene.

Thoroughbred & Classic Cars
Quadrant House
The Quadrant
Sutton, Surrey SM2 5AS
England
published monthly
This is one of the best classic car magazines in the world. It's a little hard to find in the United States, but well worth the trouble. As you would expect, it specializes in English cars, but also covers virtually everything in the world.

Hemmings Motor News
Box 100
Bennington, VT 05201
published monthly
This is the single best source for finding Austin-Healeys. If you aren't familiar with this publication then try a one-year subscription; it's impossible to find on the newsstand. It is all ads, printed on the cheapest paper possible, and generally runs around 500 pages. Only about four of these deal with Austin-Healeys, but the rest are still interesting. Any number of people will tell you they read every ad, every month. Well worth the money.

Road & Track
1499 Monrovia
Newport Beach, CA 92663
(714) 646-4455
published monthly

This is the oldest sports car magazine published in the United States. In the course of the publication's history, every Austin-Healey model has been written about at one time or another. If you have an Austin-Healey, *Road & Track* has written an article on it.

Practical Classics
90 Wickham Road
Beckenham
Kent, England
published monthly

This is a newer magazine being published in England by Paul Skilleter. It is very hard to find in the United States, but well worth the effort. There's been very little on the big Healeys in the magazine (remember the big Healeys are rare in England), but there's been a lot of Sprite and Midget material.

AUSTIN-HEALEY CLUBS

Austin-Healey Club
171 Coldharbour Road
Bristol, BS6 7SX
England

This is the major English club with over 1,200 members. It was founded in 1951 and serves the full range of Austin-Healey owners, including Sprite owners. Members publish a quarterly magazine, *The Rev Counter*, as well as regional newsletters.

Association of Jensen Owners
800 Maywood Ave
Maywood, NJ 07607

This club deals with all of the Jensen models, but since the Jensen-Healey was the most popular Jensen in the United States, this is one club the Jensen-Healey owner ought to look into joining. The club publishes a magazine called the *White Lady* and offers technical advice.

Austin-Healey Club Pacific Centre
P.O. Box 6197
San Jose, CA 95150

This is the group that takes care of all the Western Healeys in the United States. It welcomes owners of all the big Healeys as well as the Sprites. Members publish a monthly magazine and sponsor an annual gathering of the faithful. The Pacific Centre is one of the largest Austin-Healey clubs in the world.

The Austin-Healey Sports & Touring Club
P.O. Box 3539
York, PA 17402

This club is active mainly in the eastern half of the United States and encourages owners of all the Healeys to be active. It has a large number of regional clubs that also sponsor local activities. These local clubs would be more than happy to help you purchase your first Austin-Healey.

Austin-Healey Club of America
603 E. Euclid
Arlington Heights, IL 60004

This is one of the largest Austin-Healey clubs in the United States and covers every region. Chuck Anderson and the entire club were very helpful in collecting material for this book. Again, this is a club you ought to join before you purchase a Healey.

PARTS & SERVICE SOURCES

Scarborough Faire
1151 Main Street
Pawtucket, RI 02860
(800) 556-6300

This is another of the BL Heritage dealers, which carries a full line of parts for all Austin-Healeys.

FASPEC
606 SE Madison Street
Portland, OR 97214
(800) 547-8788

This is one parts supplier that does it all. They love the Healeys at this place. Stan Rice has one of the world's nicest vintage racing Bugeyes. The company's been in the business for a long time and can help you with sound advice. Best of all it has new parts, used parts, reproduced parts and even whole cars.

Delta Motorsports
1119 E. Indian School Road
Phoenix, AZ 85014
(602) 265-8026

Jensen-Healey parts aren't the easiest parts to find but this store stocks as many as anyone in the United States.

r.d. enterprises
869 Jenkintown Road
Elkins Park, PA 19117
(215) 884-5203

Even though this is primarily a Lotus shop it stocks a full line of Jensen-Healey parts. The use of a Lotus engine in the Jensen-Healey prompted r.d. enterprises to stock a full range of Jensen-Healey parts.

Moss Motors Ltd.
Box MG
Goleta, CA 93116
(800) 235-6954

This store has been around for a long time. I used to buy parts for my MG TD from these people and that was a long time ago. The best deal they have going is a series of patch panels that can be welded into all of those standard rust areas on the various Healeys. They stick

mainly to the big Healeys, although they also carry some Sprite parts.

Norman Nock Imported Cars
2060 N. Wilson Way
Stockton, CA 95205
(209) 948-8767

Norm probably doesn't like to hear it but he's been around as long as the cars. He's also a former Lucas employee and if he doesn't know about the electrical system then there aren't many other people who would. If you're on the West Coast and interested in Austin-Healeys this is one place to visit.

The Austin-Healey Store
8225 Remmet
Canoga Park, CA 91304
(213) 996-5212

The Austin-Healey Store stocks a full range of parts and is especially equipped to deal with Sprite parts. It carries both NOS and reproduction parts.

Spridgets LTD.
54 St. Peters Road
Handsworth, Birmingham B20
England
021-554-2033

Spridgets LTD. claims to stock the largest selection of new, used and rebuilt parts in the UK. If it can't supply a part for your Sprite then you really have a problem.

BRP
1808 Oak
Kansas City, MO 64108
(800) 821-3767

This is the only British Motor Heritage specialist in the midwest United States. It carries Girling, Lucas and a full line of reproduction parts for all types of Austin-Healeys.

Special Interest Car Parts
1340 Hartford Ave.
Johnston, RI 02919
(800) 556-7496
(800) 851-5600

If you're having trouble locating parts, this company can help. Friends of mine in the restoration business depend on these people. They especially like the prices and the service.

Southern Carburetters
Unit 14, Oakwood Ind. Park
Gatwick Rd., Crawley
Sussex RH10 2AZ
0926-640031
This is most likely the largest Austin-Healey parts dealer in the world. These are the people to see when no one else has the part you need. If they don't have it, and don't know where to find it, give up.

Healey Surgeons
7211 Carroll Avenue
Takoma Park, MD 20912
(301) 270-8811
Bruce and Ian Phillips are probably the largest Austin-Healey restorers on the east coast. Not only will they restore your Austin-Healey but they can provide you with all the parts you'll need to do it yourself.

Hemphill's Healey Heaven
4-B Winters Lane
Baltimore, MD 21228
(301) 788-2191
These are the people that specialize in sheetmetal parts. They carry floors, outriggers, fenders, sills and shrouds. They also make a lot of the parts available in aluminum and fiberglass.

Sports & Classics
512 Boston Post Road
Darien, CT 06820
(203) 655-8731
This company carries a full range of parts for Sprites and large Healeys; also a full line of interior parts.

Seven Enterprises Ltd.
716 Bluecrab Road
Newport News, VA 23606
(800) 992-7007
These folks have helped me put together a number of Minis. They've now branched out to handling Sprite parts. They not only charge fair prices but they have one of the largest inventories of Sprite engine parts in the country.

A-H Spares Ltd.
Unit 7, Southam Industrial Estate
Southam, Warwickshire CV33 OJH
It stocks a comprehensive line of spare parts for both Austin-Healey and Jensen-Healey. The company also ships worldwide.